MY HEROES
and Their Stories of
SURVIVAL

Patrick J. Bastow, DDS.

CONTENTS

DEDICATION

This book is dedicated to all the men and women who have honorably served our country defending our freedom.

A portion of the proceeds will be donated to Veterans organizations.

ACKNOWLEDGEMENTS

David Ragusa – Editor, retired English teacher, and friend

James Peterson – Technical support, final assembly of manuscript, former patient

Kenneth Buschner- Photographic support, owner B-25 studios, and friend

Special thanks to my wife Deborah and daughter Ashley for assistance throughout this process

INTRODUCTION

As John peered out the window at the snow falling, the
smile slowly drained from his face. His memories of the war in Europe
always returned during the first winter snowfall. This would never change.

John always appeared happy such as when he shared with me the story
of his recent wedding anniversary celebration at the American Legion.
Knowing how much he loved to dance had prompted the family to hire a
band and play the "old tunes" for dancing. As a young man, he wanted to
meet more young ladies at the USO dances so he had taken dancing lessons
while on leave after basic training. He felt that becoming a good dancer
would improve his luck with the ladies and he was correct.

He had been very patriotic when he joined the Army and wanted to
get into combat as soon as possible. John wanted to "shoot some Germans"
and help win the war. His wish came true as he found himself freezing
in the snow shrouded forests of Belgium. It was dark but John could see
movement against the white background in the distance. He knew this was
where the enemy soldiers were. This was his chance to finally kill his first
Nazi. Slowly he raised his rifle and took careful aim at the human form. A
shot rang out. The man dropped into the snow. John was thrilled and could
not wait until dawn so he could walk out there and check out "his kill". He
approached slowly in case more enemy soldiers were hiding nearby until
he stood over the lifeless body. The German soldier was not much more
than a boy with a full head of blonde hair. John searched the soldier and
soon found his wallet. He read the soldier's name, one he would never forget. Then he discovered a photo of the young man, standing proudly with

three other people- obviously his parents and younger sister. This was a real person from a loving family he had killed.

John looked out the window of my office and soon tears began to roll down his cheeks. He looked at me again and said, "Killing that young man really did not make any difference determining the outcome of the war. This memory has haunted me ever since."

Many years ago, I was asked to work at a nearby mall and provide oral cancer screenings as part of a senior citizen's health fair. As a dentist working for the Veterans Administration I was more than willing to participate in any community service when asked to do so.

It was there where Irving, another veteran, strolled up and requested an examination. "Certainly, "was my reply. "Please have a seat."

I was very surprised to see that he was missing many of his teeth but only on one side.

"How may I ask did this happen?" I said as I stepped back.

"I was shot in the face during the war." Irv responded.

"Why hasn't this been treated at the VA?"I asked.

Irving replied, "When I was discharged I was given the runaround by the government so I never asked for help after that."

I replied firmly, "Well, from now on you will be taken care of. I will see to that."

Our doctor patient relationship began that day, but that relationship evolved over time to one of genuine respect and friendship. It was necessary for Irv to drive some distance to his appointments and so later on this included having lunch together. On one such lunch, we were talking about the care he had received in the field hospital in Italy after being wounded when he abruptly shifted the conversation.

Irv began, "General Patton visited the hospital one day to speak with the injured soldiers and stopped in front of one with no apparent wounds. The man was obviously suffering from battle fatigue and would not talk,"

Irv said. He continued telling the story. "Patton asked, 'What's wrong with you soldier?' The man buried his face in his hands and said he couldn't stand it anymore. General Patton then slapped the man and called him a coward."

Irv was angry and he said, "What a terrible thing to do! Patton had no idea what that man had gone through." I wish that Irv was still around to share more of his stories, but he, like so many of his peers, is no longer with us.

Another veteran, Stanley, hailed from Brooklyn and also volunteered to serve his country but never believed combat was as bad as others had suggested. He found himself in the Ardennes in early December of 1944, but was inadequately prepared for such miserable weather. With only a shirt and field jacket to protect him from the cold, it was inevitable that he would soon suffer with frostbitten hands and feet. Stanley remembers the combat vividly: shooting, being shot at, and freezing all the while. After several days of fighting, the food and ammunition began to run low and he, along with eight other soldiers, became separated from his unit. They wandered aimlessly in the snowy forest for days, frightened, freezing, and with declining food supplies. After a few more days, the food and ammunition were gone and their spirits were broken. The group ran into a number of German soldiers because they had wandered behind enemy lines. Unable to fight any longer, they were forced to surrender. Stanley and his compatriots somehow would survive the next several months as prisoners of war eating rutabagas, an occasional potato and uncooked turnips they dug up along the road.

Years later Stanley would say, "The fear and anguish of combat were beyond imagination." Somehow he suppressed these memories until the first war in Iraq began. The start of that military campaign was a trigger for him and many other combat veterans I spoke with over the years. They needed help and for many this would be their first time hearing that they were suffering from Post-Traumatic Stress Disorder (PTSD).

For the past 38 years, I have helped care for disabled American veterans with as much compassion as possible while working at the V.A. Hospital in Canandaigua, N.Y. During that time, older veterans, from World War II, increasingly began to share their stories with me. It is possible that memories buried so long become less painful and threatening.

The fact that they felt comfortable with me probably contributed to their willingness to share their stories. I recall speaking with a psychologist from the PTSD clinic one afternoon and he mentioned that frequently the veterans have dental appointments prior to coming to his clinic. The psychologist went on to say, "The guys often say that they don't need to talk with me today after seeing the dentist. You must be doing something right." I was honored when they wanted to share their experiences with me, experiences that in some cases they had not ever shared with their families.

I began to be invited to various functions such as the annual Ex-Prisoners of War Christmas party and MIA/POW recognition day for which I was asked to be the keynote speaker on two occasions. It was at one such event that a couple of the veterans suggested that I do something with the material they had shared with me. Many had already provided me with newspaper articles and photographs. All that remained was the need an interview to link the events together. So began this "labor of love" for me where I have attempted to capture both the facts and feelings of these men and women who remain my heroes. They sacrificed so much to guarantee our freedom, a freedom many unfortunately today take for granted.

I would be remiss if I did not mention the devoted and compassionate people who worked with me during my career serving our veterans. They recognized the sacrifices made by the veteran and how this impacted the veterans' lives. The quality of care I was able to provide was in many ways due to this support received from these men and women.

VA Clinic Waiting Room

Seated: (l-r) Bob Baker, Bob Botash, Tony Nardone, Albert Pistilli
Standing: dental assistant Mary Lee Hurlburt, and the Author

A WAGER --ANTHONY NARDONE

"This war will be over by Christmas," the young man said emphatically.

"No it won't," was the response of a second man standing nearby.

A wager was about to be made between two Allied prisoners of war during the fall of 1944. Their home for the duration of World War II would be Stalag Luft I in northern Germany along with nearly 25,000 other airmen. All Tony Nardone wanted to do as a teenager was to play guitar in a band and chase young women. Little did he know that before realizing his dream of going to college, he would be confined behind barbed wire in a German prison camp.

He had been born on August 24, 1923, in Rochester, New York, the son of parents who had emigrated from Italy. After graduating from high school in June of 1941, he joined a band with ten other boys and began to make some real money. He thought that this would come in handy later paying for college.

The United States entered World War II in December of 1941, with the bombing of Pearl Harbor. This development would change his plans. When he turned 19 in 1942, a notice was sent out that the Army Air Corps was looking for young men who would qualify for training to ultimately fly in combat missions. Previously, a minimum of two years of college had been required. But with the losses already sustained, things had changed. An equivalency test could be taken that was very difficult with only a small percentage of the young men passing. His name was called and he assumed that he, along with a few others, had failed. This was not the case however. Unfortunately, he would need his mother's signature but she refused. She did not want to be responsible for something happening to him.

Tony said, "If you don't sign and I get drafted and possibly die...." So she signed reluctantly.

In January of 1943, he was ordered to report for duty and traveled to Atlantic City, New Jersey. There the young men drilled in their civilian clothing because of the uniform shortage. While he was not allowed to have his guitar for the six weeks of basic training, Tony was able to enjoy the entertainment provided to the soldiers that included the Glenn Miller band.

Tony was transferred to Indianapolis, Indiana where he studied mathematics, chemistry and other courses, but now also began actually flying in planes. There were 10 hours of flying time with instructors and periodic examinations to qualify for the next phase of training known as "flight school".

The Classification Center in Nashville, Tennessee, would determine what role these young men finishing flight school were best suited for. There were tests involving motor skills and physical evaluations. Tony was asked if being a first-generation Italian in the United States would affect his ability to bomb Italy if need be. He responded that he definitely could.

Tests were administered to determine each candidate's suitability as a pilot, navigator or bombardier. Tony scored 9/10 on each of the three exams. He felt that being a pilot would be boring with the autopilot technology available and the same could be said of the bombardier position. The job of the navigator seemed to be more challenging and interesting and this was ultimately his choice.

After a brief stay in Louisiana, he was on his way to Fort Myers, Florida, for gunnery school. All members of the crew would need to be proficient in this area. They all learned to fire rifles, machine guns, and the 45 caliber handgun, but the most interesting was the shotgun training intended to teach men how to lead and hit a moving target. While riding the back of a truck that took the cadet through a 26 mile course, he was asked to hit clay pigeons that were launched from hidden locations. It was actually fun using the double barrel shotgun and shooting at these fast targets. Tony soon became quite skilled at this.

Learning to hit moving targets was important for the next phase when he practiced hitting a long sleeve that was being towed behind a C-47 transport plane while he rode in the back seat of an AT-6 trainer. The 30 caliber machine guns spent casings were caught in a canvas bag attached to the gun. On one occasion, a cadet did not have the zipper closed and some of the spent brass casings hit the head of the instructor seated just in front of him.

After being hit several times, the instructor finally had had enough and hollered, "Save your brass!" But the student thought he said, "Save your ass!" and immediately bailed out of the plane.

After he received his "gunnery wings", it was back to Monroe, Louisiana, for advanced navigation training. There were several navigational aids that were utilized when flying: pilotage, dead reckoning, use of radio compass (using call letters broadcast from cities nearby) and celestial aids.

This last technique required the use of a sextant and used stars to aid in navigation. While this was stressed in the training, it would ultimately be of little use in Europe where the bombing missions by the United States were conducted during the daytime.

While on a training mission to Texas, the plane directly in front of his, with students and instructors aboard, crashed while landing and the entire crew was killed. Training accidents unfortunately resulted in many fatalities during the war.

In April of 1942, Tony was sent to Avon Park, Florida, and was finally assigned to a crew that consisted of 10 men. The pilot, copilot, navigator, and bombardier were all officers. Completing the crew was a tail gunner, two waist gunners, a radio operator, an engineer, and the ball turret gunner.

This latter group were enlisted men. They were assigned a plane and were scheduled to take a new B-17 to England when the tail gunner known as "Tex" got sick. Their plane was unfortunately given to another crew for the journey and Tony's crew had to endure crossing the Atlantic Ocean on a luxury liner will all the comforts of home.

After a 10 day journey to Birmingham, England, he joined the 351st Bomb Group, 511th Squadron in Polebrook. Three other squadrons, the 508th, 509th, and 510th, each with 12 planes, were part of the 351st bomb group. They were now members of General Doolittle's Eighth Air Force, called the "Mighty Eighth".

The first plane his crew was assigned was a B-17 E without a nose turret for added protection. They flew five combat missions on this plane and were then given a new B-17 G with a nose turret (two additional machine guns). His old plane was taken over by a new crew that unfortunately crashed on its second mission.

Tony will never forget any of his missions, but the first was on his 21st birthday when they bombed a German submarine base at Weimer. Their objective was to destroy the enemy's war making capability. Enemy troops, equipment, factories, and refineries were all targets assigned on their daylight missions. The British planes bombed at night and were more indiscriminate with their objectives.

All airmen had been trained on how to strap on a parachute while in the plane. They were also instructed to delay opening the parachute as long as possible if forced to bail out of the plane. While flying at 28,000 feet, there is little oxygen and it could be as cold as -70 degrees Fahrenheit.

Upon learning this, Tony prayed. "Please Lord, don't let me ever have to bail out."

On their third mission a plane nearby received a direct hit and exploded.

Seeing this Tony prayed again. "Lord, please give me a chance to bail out."

The non-pressurized B-17 offered very little protection to the crew inside. The men wore electric flying suits that plugged into a power source and oxygen masks. Along with a payload of up to 4000 pounds of bombs, there were 3000 gallons of gasoline, 10,000 rounds of 50 caliber ammunition, and an oxygen tank. The whole plane was an explosive device. Even when assigned a "milk run", where little resistance was expected, the take off with such a load was still frightening.

A B-17 could fly up to 3000 miles and cruise at 180mph. Most missions included several hundred bombers and Tony recalls one mission where there were 1200 planes attacking the Third Reich.

The day of a mission began at around 2 a.m. with a briefing. The target was identified and information about antiaircraft sites and weather conditions was provided. After a substantial breakfast, it was time to board the aircraft and prepare for takeoff. During 1944, Tony flew missions on August 24, August 25, August 30, September 5, September 8, September 9, September 10, September 11 and September 12. Occasionally there were at least a couple of days to unwind between these stressful missions. What was experienced by most men was terrifying and some of them never recovered from the trauma. The losses sustained by the Eighth Air Force during World War II were considerable. It was likely you would eventually either be a casualty or shot down and captured by the enemy.

It was not until many years after the war had ended that Tony learned that only men that served on submarines suffered a higher percentage of casualties.

For the eighth mission, their plane was scheduled to be the camera ship that would photograph and report damage inflicted during the mission. This plane flew in the middle the formation and was therefore well protected. Once the mission was completed, they were required to return promptly with this information so it would be available when the other crews were being debriefed.

After completing the bomb run, however, the pilot, Claude, immediately pulled the plane out of formation and tried to make it back to England without consulting his navigator. An argument quickly ensued. The pilot got lost and put the crew in great danger for they no longer had the protection from the other planes on the mission. They arrived home after most of the other planes had already landed. During debriefing, both Tony and the pilot said that they had no excuses for being late returning to England. Afterward, Tony threatened to never fly with Claude again because of the danger he had subjected his crew to. Somehow things were smoothed out, but because of their failure on this last mission they were assigned a terrible location known as "tail end Charlie" for the following mission where they would be much more exposed and vulnerable to attacking enemy fighters.

There were two objectives for the next mission: to attract enemy their supporting fighters could engage them and destroy an oil depot near fighters so the Polish border on the east side of Germany. While near Berlin, however, the enemy fighters attacked. The report stated that between 35 and 60 FW190s and ME109s participated. These enemy planes attacked two at a time to confuse the gunners on the B-17s.

Understand that, during wartime, only a fraction of servicemen actually experience real combat. Most are assigned the responsibility of providing support for the men on the front lines but still are eligible for care at the VA after discharge. This might explain the reaction of several other veterans seated in my waiting room one day several years ago when Tony shared a vivid description of his experience in their presence.

"The waist gunner would say things like, 'Fighters at 1000 yards, fighters at 500 yards, fighters preparing to board' – but then he was killed. The sound of the machine gun fire, the plane's engines roaring and the enemy cannon shells hitting the fuselage was deafening. It was like being in a garbage can while someone hit the outside with a hammer. The plane was on fire now and out of control at 28,000 feet. The pilot rang the bell eight times

- the signal to bail out, but the escape hatch was jammed. I began to stomp on it and it suddenly gave way with me cascading out into total silence."

You could hear a pin drop in the waiting room as the other veterans listened with their mouths agape.

He shared the remainder of his story with me several weeks later.

"The landing was hard and soon I was surrounded by threatening civilians brandishing pitchforks and shotguns. Luckily a kid in uniform arrived, probably a Hitler youth, and told the others that I was his prisoner. After being stripped and searched I was placed in a locked bunker."

"The next day I was joined by four other prisoners and five German guards who escorted us and a dead airman in a wagon. We walked into Berlin and were placed on a wood-burning streetcar. There was some semblance of humanity as one of the guards offered me a portion of his ration; a piece of bread and some greasy sausage. I had not eaten anything since boarding my plane for the mission the previous morning. What I remember the most about this experience was the utter devastation in Berlin and the people walking hunched over among the rubble."

In Frankfurt, Tony was interrogated by his captors but gave only his name, rank and serial number as instructed during training in spite of their threats. He recalls a guard there playing a tune on an accordion that he recognized. He asked if they had a guitar. And then for a few minutes they played a duet together in spite of being adversaries.

The men were next loaded into a boxcar bound for Barth, in northern Germany. The next 72 hours were a nightmare. There was severe congestion in the boxcar and the train was periodically strafed by Allied fighters during the trip. Each time the train was attacked while stopped, the guards would flee and leave the prisoners locked inside.

All of my patients who are former prisoners have told me this was amongst the most terrifying experience they endured because they were utterly defenseless even from their own forces.

Once they arrived at Stalag Luft I, the prisoners were deloused, showered, and placed in barracks. Tony's barracks had 15 individual rooms with 14 men in each. There were four compounds in the prison camp. His held 2500 men. Over time there were 24 men crammed into his particular room.

The conditions there were not good but at least they were alive. They had some food that included the weekly Red Cross parcels and they were treated to a shower every other week. There was a roll call each morning and afterword the prisoners were allowed to walk around the compound. They knew not to cross that single strand of barbed wire just inside the high fence. Entering no man's land would result in a prisoner being immediately shot. A few of the prisoners were placed in solitary confinement for various offenses but otherwise they were treated humanely.

The men amused themselves in several ways. Music was the thing that helped Tony pass the time as a prisoner. There were some instruments provided by the Red Cross that included a guitar, a saxophone and a trombone. Tony was able to form a small band and entertain the other prisoners. They were called "Tony Nardone and His Skins of Appeal". He was surprised to find that three of his roommates were also from Rochester, New York: Bob Ayett, Ed Wilkins and Pat Scarpino. These last two men mentioned were coincidentally also patients of mine.

By January, 1945, Red Cross parcels ceased to be delivered and the prisoners continued to lose weight. The mental torment from the crowding and poor sanitation began to wear on the captives. Tony credits his strong faith as the most important factor in his surviving this ordeal.

The prison camp was finally liberated by the Russians in April of 1945 and the men were airlifted back to Le Havre, France. One day, Tony and two other liberated prisoners were walking to a general meeting and they passed another soldier with what appeared to be corporal's insignia. As they passed, however, they noticed that it was in fact five stars and quickly saluted. This soldier was none other than Dwight D Eisenhower, the Supreme Allied Commander.

Ike said. "Where are you from?"

"Rochester, New York," Tony replied.

"I was there once and stayed at the Sheraton Hotel-a nice city," the General responded.

He also spoke with the other men present and then continued on his way for he was the main speaker at the meeting.

Tony returned home on the elegant Queen Elizabeth and on one of his many walks around the ship, noticed an Army Chaplin seated alone near a checker board. Recalling his days as the #9 School playground champion, he asked the captain if he wanted to play a game or two. The chaplain replied, "Sure."

Tony thought, "I've got a live one here," but after only two moves he was beaten. Tony tried once more and was trounced again after only two moves. "I can't understand it," he moaned. "I was the #9 School playground champion."

The chaplain looked at Tony and said, "I was the checker champion at Ohio State."

Soon after arriving in his hometown of Rochester, New York, Tony married Grace. They raised three wonderful children. He received his degree in mechanical engineering from the University Rochester and worked for several companies over the years. Tony retired from Kodak in 1962 and then also retired from the reserves with the rank of Lieutenant Colonel.

"I have been volunteering for the past thirty years", Tony recently told me. "I design and fabricate special devices for people with disabilities." This community service was the subject of an article featured in the local newspaper a few years ago.

Years later Tony would be invited to participate in the "Honor Flight" to Washington, DC and a visit to the World War II Memorial. While walking down the street he passed another elderly veteran who looked familiar.

It was his bombardier Gus. He hollered, "Gus!" A crowd gathered as the two men embraced with tears in their eyes.

As for the wager made by those two airmen so many years ago, we all know who won. But did he ever collect?

Tony chuckles whenever he tells the following story. "When the day finally arrived, Christmas Day, 1944, the colonel asked permission after roll call for the men to collect on the bet. Each man had a second to assist him like fighters have for a fight. In front of the entire formation, nearly 2,500 witnesses, the winner dropped his drawers and the loser cleaned his behind. Powder was then applied for visual proof of contact made between the lips of the loser," the kisser", and the butt of the winner or " kissee". When the loser kissed the ass of the winner, both the prisoners and the guards laughed hysterically."

Everyone who ever served in combat recalls humorous events such as this. I think in some ways this is a blessing for it helps to dull the painful memories of war.

I had heard much of Tony's fascinating story in the form of snippets shared over several years, such as the waiting room narrative. It was necessary to tie this all together so arrangements were made to interview and record the information. He and I were seated at his kitchen table and it was noon. We were ready to begin when Tony turned to his wife, Grace and said, "Could we have some coffee?"

A hot cup was poured for both of us and he began speaking. After what seemed to be a short while, Tony stopped and took a sip and said, "Grace, this coffee is cold!"

I looked up at the clock. It was 2 p.m. He had been talking for two straight hours! Grace turned in his direction and calmly replied, "Tony, it was hot when I filled your cup."

Today when someone uses the word "hero" around Tony he corrects them. "It was my job. I did what I had to do." Most of us would beg to differ.

Tony standing with the crew of his B-17. Tony is standing second from left.

Photograph of young Tony affixed to his prisoner records.

Tony Nardone and his wife Grace, in their home in Rochester, NY.

THE PIPE —BOB BOTASH

The year was 1944 and Bob's parents had just received the dreaded telegram from the War Department. Their only son was now missing in action. Their worst fears had been realized. Months would pass before there was any more information and they both assumed the worst.

Robert Botash was born in Rochester, New York, and after a brief stay in Buffalo the family returned. He remembers vividly that Sunday afternoon when his family had company for dinner. Bob had gone into the other room and was listening to the radio and the end of a special announcement. "As soon as more information comes in, we will relay this to you."

Since it was December, Bob naturally concluded that this was just another warning of an approaching storm until he heard the rest of the broadcast. He was correct in a way for a storm of Japanese planes had just rained bombs on the U.S. fleet at Pearl Harbor. This was his last year in high school and soon some of his teachers began to leave after joining the service. He began to realize the significance of the war when gas and food rationing started. Even empty toothpaste tubes had to be turned in to purchase a new tube. Window shades had to be closed when the blackout sirens wailed. Life had changed for America and would remain so for several years.

Bob graduated from high school and had started college at the University of Buffalo when his draft notice arrived. He requested a deferment so he could complete his first year of school. His last examination was completed on May 14 and he received his induction notice on the following day. Bob took an exam to determine whether he qualified for advanced training and possibly officer's candidate school in the U.S. Army. He passed and was ordered to report to Fort Niagara near Buffalo, New York. Bob recalls the day when his father drove him to the train station, but stopped in route to make a special purchase. He bought his son a pipe and tobacco and said, "You're now old enough to smoke."

For most of us, the initial separation from a child, usually the oldest, can be traumatic. Today, this occurs most often when the child leaves for college. I can only imagine parents' feelings during the war when their son left not knowing if they would ever see him again.

Several years ago, Bob came in for his dental visit and he noticed that I was in a somber mood. I told him that my wife, Debbie, and I had taken our son to college the previous day and were heartbroken. I will never forget the moment when we were standing outside his dorm and our son said, "Mom, Dad, it's time for you to leave."

Bob smiled and told me that he and his wife had similar feelings when they left their son off at Cornell University. It was ironic that he was now consoling me, the same person who as an only child had left his parents so many years ago and gone off to war.

After two weeks at Fort Niagara, Bob was transferred to Fort McClellan in Alabama for basic training. Bob quickly learned that he might be treated differently in the south when the drill instructor asked, "How many of you are from up north?"

"The northerners were ordered to jog around the track fifteen times while the rest of the men watched," Bob remembers clearly.

For three grueling weeks, they were all "asses and elbows" as they say in the Army. This is an old military expression suggesting that this is all that should be visible when a man is truly exerting himself. By the end of this training, Bob was able to hike for 25 miles, a feat not everyone could accomplish.

After a furlough, Bob was sent to the Citadel in Charleston, South Carolina, where he began his studies. It was now August of 1943. He lived in one of the dorms and felt like he was in college again. He completed two abbreviated semesters that ended in January. The advanced engineering training that he anticipated did not happen and instead he was sent to Fort Bragg, North Carolina. Here he joined the 100th Infantry Division.

He recalls seeing a movie describing how one should act if they were captured by the enemy. "Show military courtesy, provide your name, rank and serial number, and never ever be a wise guy."

The regular camp commander went on furlough and his replacement placed Bob on a list of men who would serve as replacements in the ETO or European Theater of Operation.

After a brief stay in Washington, DC where the men received gas mask training, it was on to Boston to begin their journey across the dangerous Atlantic. The converted cruise ship they were on was escorted by a large blimp that searched for German U boats, but it discontinued shadowing them after only two days. The voyage was therefore a tension filled trip.

As they neared England, escort ships arrived to provide some protection until they docked in Liverpool. Once ashore, one of the first advertisements he saw was a Kodak billboard that was a welcome sight for this young man from Rochester, New York. "Jolly Good Snaps" it read.

The train to Southampton made a brief stop where several young ladies were passing out coffee and doughnuts to the men. Bob thought this would be the first English girl that he met and asked one, "Where are you from?"

She replied, "Brooklyn."

This encounter confirmed that the whole country was now involved in the war effort

In September their ship anchored just off of Omaha Beach in Normandy, France. All was quiet for this landing three months after D-Day. As they crested the hill, however, he was greeted by a sobering sight - thousands of white crosses for the boys who had died there on June 6. The replacement soldiers did not have any weapons when they landed. A large dump truck soon arrived and dumped the load of rifles onto the ground. Bob selected what looked like a good quality rifle, but once he took it to the range he found that he was unable to hit the target. Each time he fired a red flag went up. "Maggie's drawers", the nickname for the red flag, indicated a clear miss. Bob had qualified as a sharpshooter in basic training and could not believe he was missing so badly.

A frustrated officer asked for the rifle and said, "Let me show you how to use this."

The officer also missed the target and concluded that the sights must be off. The defective weapon was turned in. Two days later, the rest of his platoon was sent off to join Patton's army, but he was left behind. His reward for not qualifying with a rifle was one week's kitchen police duty better known as KP. Finally he was assigned to a new company and given a gun that someone said "should work". This was reassuring. Bob never had a chance to test fire the gun and now was moving up to the front lines.

A truck took them to St. Lo, France, where nearly all of the buildings had been destroyed. He was sickened when he saw a lady walk out of her nearly demolished home and wave to the men. The residents were obviously in good spirits since the Allied forces had liberated them from the Nazi oppression.

They next boarded a train and passed through Paris. After riding for two more days, they entered Belgium. Here the men would join the 9th Infantry Division as replacements. Each man was given 240 rounds of ammunition and two grenades as they passed through the now breached Siegfried line. Bob began to notice dead livestock strewn about. Soon there were human bodies, both German and American, laying everywhere. They did not look real. They looked like wax figures. These men had been alive, however, just a few days before. Seeing all these bodies was a "sight he would never forget." For three consecutive days he had to follow a certain path to get C rations for the men. Each day he had to step over the body of an American soldier. Sadly Bob noticed the young man was wearing a wedding band.

What Bob was joining was the Battle of the Hürtgen Forest, soon to become one of the bloodiest conflicts of World War II. In this dark and nearly impenetrable region of Germany, his division would suffer 4500 casualties over the next three months. Overall there were 33,000 Allied casualties during this time.

This battle finally ended when the Germans attacked in the southern Ardennes on December 16th, the beginning of the "Battle of the Bulge."

Bob recalls covering the foxholes with pine branches to shield the men from shrapnel from artillery shells exploding overhead. He says he never met an atheist there; all the men were praying to survive this ordeal.

On one particular patrol they were directed to cross a road and dig in. They sauntered across, convinced the enemy was not nearby. They were wrong. The men had walked into an ambush. The Germans opened up and the men hit the deck. They began to return fire but could not really see the well concealed enemy. His assistant platoon leader nearby started to say something to him and was immediately hit the face. He was still alive and began to crawl on his hands and knees with blood streaming down his face. Each time one of the men tried running back across the road, a machine gun opened fire. Soon he could hear their moans.

Around six o'clock it began to get dark and Bob wandered around for a while. Since he could not see anything, he decided to stay put. When dawn arrived, Bob slowly stood up and looked around. Now there was a row of rifles pointing at him. He still doesn't know why they didn't shoot him immediately. One of the Germans said, "For you the war is over." It was December 17, 1944, and he was now their prisoner.

As he was being taken back through their lines a German soldier younger than he asked, "Haben Sie cigarette?"

Bob gave his pack to the young German who only took one and then handed it back. He motioned for Bob to have one also so they sat down and smoked together. This was unbelievable Bob thought. Yesterday they had been trying to kill one other.

They were soon joined by some other German soldiers and one said in perfect English "Where are you from?"

Bob replied, "Rochester, New York."

The German soldier said that he was from Brooklyn and had worked with his brother in a store there. He produced a picture of a young G.I. and said that that was his brother. "Do you know him?"

An officer arrived and began showing the other men how to operate a machine gun as Bob stood by watching. Soon a second officer began to question him, but Bob provided limited information as he had been trained. Bob conceded that he was a member of the Ninth Division since they already knew this. He was wearing a 9th Division patch on his uniform.

Bob was taken to a house and questioned further. He noticed a bowl of apples and pears on the table. The German who had been interrogating him left the room. Since he had not eaten for two days he was starving. Was this a trick? He was afraid to touch the fruit. Soon an older lady entered the room and proceeded to place an apple and pear in each of his two pockets. She obviously felt some pity for this young man, and he was grateful.

He was placed in the loft of a barn and given a bowl of black water, which he assumed was their coffee, some rutabaga/turnip soup, and a piece of moldy bread. This was actually a whole day's ration for a German soldier he later learned. Two more prisoners were added and soon the group had grown to ten men. These last two had strange accents and he suspected they were "plants" to obtain more information. "We never thought to ask them questions about the American pastime, baseball," he said.

A farmer brought them food a couple of times and Bob really appreciated the bread with jam that he was given. It was so much better than the moldy bread that he had received from the guard. The group of captured GIs now numbered close to 25 and they were directed by the guards to search for canned food in a bombed out area. The prisoners were searched to see if they were attempting to steal any of the food. Bob managed to conceal one can and saved it for later hoping that it would possibly contain some meat. Once he opened the can, however, he smelled something he had never been able to stand as a boy, spinach. Even though he was very hungry he could not eat it. None of the other men ate it either.

The prisoners walked at least 25 km to Limburg and Stalag 12a. Reaching the train line, about 60 of the men were crammed into a boxcar intended for no more than forty people or eight horses. There was a slop bucket in the center of the car for the men to relieve themselves. You were lucky if you had a place to sit where you could lean against the wooden side of the box car. Otherwise you were pushed by the other men as the train moved along. Once you moved to use the slop bucket however someone else would have taken your place. The door was opened once each day to empty the slop bucket. After eight days in this dark, smelly, congested car, the men were ready to kill one another. Any prisoner who was ever transported in one of these boxcars said it was a horrible experience.

Once they entered New Brandenburg, the prisoners disembarked and began marching through the town. The civilians shook their fists and spat upon them. This new prison camp, Stalag I2a, housed GIs who were enlisted men. Bob joined about 100 other men who were taken to another compound where they would be forced to work. Red Cross parcels normally intended for one man per week were shared between four prisoners.

On one occasion while the men were shoveling dirt, Bob threw a shovel full directly behind him. All the men gasped and stop working. He had thrown the dirt directly into the chest of the German guard. Bob was sure he would be shot this time and quickly ran over to the older man and brushed him off. The guard looked sternly at Bob and then finally smiled. They were human beings after all.

In February of 1945 they returned to New Brandenburg, not to the main camp but a new worksite. The smaller compound held nearly 100 prisoners and again they were forced to work all day long. Bob recalls one day when he had a toothache and he was taken to see another prisoner who happened to be a French dentist. This man provided some relief with very primitive equipment. Regardless of the camp where they were held, all the men were subjected to the bites of the lice that infested their straw mattresses.

One day, a guard passed out postcards to all the prisoners and instructed them to fill them out. The cards would be mailed to their families back home they were told. And February 27, 1945, his dad received Bob's card in the mail. His son was alive. After three months of anguish, the most wonderful news a parent could ever wish for finally arrived. Thank God!

By this time the men were starving from the meager rations of food they had. The black bread that contained sawdust and rutabagas/turnip soup would never replace the meals their mothers had cooked. They no longer dreamed of girls like most young men did. Now they dreamed of food instead. The men became obsessed with the thought of food and talked about nothing else.

One spring day, a guard arrived and said. "Boys, gather your things together. We are leaving camp tonight."

The prisoners could see Russian aircraft attacking in the distance. The enemy was closing in. The prisoners marched for several days only stopping to sleep on the ground at night. The guards finally realized that it was over and threw their weapons away. They said that they would surrender to the American soldiers for they were terrified of the Russians.

The prisoners were now on their own and began to wander about in small groups. They were hungry and filthy. Bob had worn the same clothes for nearly 7 months and during that time he had had only one shower. Five of the men stuck together and walked until one day they spotted a Red Cross truck approaching. The driver knew where the American troops were and reluctantly said he would drive them there. After riding for a while Bob could see an American tank approaching with a GI perched on top. Bob remembers this as one of the "three high points of his in his life." He was finally free!

A week later, with a clean uniform and some real GI food in his stomach, he was transported to "Camp Lucky Strike" in Le Havre, France. As he walked around he noticed a B-17 with men standing around it. He immediately recognized the pilot as a friend of his from grammar school. Another GI watching the plane stood nearby and he was also very familiar. It was his cousin Bill. He tapped him on the shoulder and when Bill looked around he said, "What are you doing here?" His cousin had also been captured in the Battle of the Bulge.

Bob would return to Rochester, get married and complete college. He and his wife Mary were blessed with four children. A long successful career in education culminated with him being selected to be the principal of Churchville Chili High School. He retired from this position in 1985.

The days of forced labor, filthy clothing, lice infested bedding and poor sanitation are now distant memories. He told me, his dentist, once that "I was not a hero; just a lucky survivor."

Mr. Botash came to the VA Dental Clinic one morning several years ago carrying a package with a special souvenir from the war. Carefully he opened the box and a produced a faded yet original Nazi flag. Looking at this black swastika against the red background sent chills down my spine. I was so stunned that I actually was afraid to touch it.

Bob suggested that I show the flag to my staff. I did more than that. I walked slowly to the hospital director's office. A few of the younger clerical staff looked puzzled but one finally asked, "What's that?" "That, young lady, is the reason why you have a job serving the veterans," I responded.

Recently Bob told me about a trip he and his cousin, also a former POW, took to his uncle's farm in Indiana just after returning home from the war. When they sat down for dinner just after arriving, his uncle said to his wife, "Honey, what do you have for the boys?" She proudly placed a huge pot of soup on the table. Rutabaga soup! The boys both began to laugh. Bob Botash, like every other veteran of World War II, never complained about serving his country, with one exception. He would "rather die than ever have another bowl of rutabaga soup!"

Bob shortly after joining the army smoking the pipe.

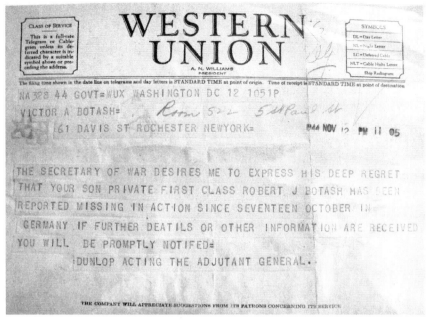

Telegram notifying Bobs's parents that their son was MIA.

Postcard from prison camp notifying Bob's parents that he was alive.

Bob holding a souvenir of his experiences in Germany.

A NURSE – SUE GRIFFEN

Susan Griffin sat quietly in the dental chair waiting for her appointment to begin when my dental assistant said, "Doc is going to have surgery on his hand."

She grasped my left hand and after a brief inspection said, "Oh honey, nobody ever died from Dupuytren's."

What a profound statement that was. After her experiences in Okinawa during World War II, my condition seemed so insignificant.

Sue was born in Canandaigua, New York, in 1921, and lived there until she completed high school in Manchester, New York. She was interested in becoming a registered nurse, and at the age of 17, departed for nursing school in Buffalo, New York. She began her training at E.J. Meyer Memorial Hospital and completed the program in three years.

The world around her was rapidly changing as aggressive regimes in Europe and in the Pacific signaled the end to her peaceful life. The attack on Pearl Harbor finally dragged the United States into this bloody conflict that would ultimately take the lives of millions of people.

She answered the call to duty as many other young people did in the early 1940's and enlisted in the Army. After several weeks of basic training, and time at Fort Lewis, she was transferred to Atlantic City, New Jersey, where she cared for injured servicemen returning from Europe.

She quickly learned that when you entered a ward full of injured soldiers, the first thing you had to do was to announce your presence by saying,

"I'm the nurse." Injured patients who might be sleeping could possibly attack the staff if they were awakened suddenly. These men were already showing evidence of the shock and trauma from experiencing combat.

With time she became more comfortable caring for these injured soldiers, but she soon received orders that she was going to be transferred. After traveling across the United States by train, Sue boarded a ship bound for Okinawa. Okinawa is a small island 350 miles from the southernmost portion of Japan and an important stepping stone for the Allied forces as they prepared to invade Japan. The people there were a very diverse population since the island had come under the control of the Japanese in 1875. Unfortunately, the Japanese considered these civilians to be inferior and treated them as such.

When the battle for Okinawa commenced, the civilians were caught in a crossfire between the Allied forces and the retreating Japanese Third Army. These people have been taught to fear the Americans, and believed our soldiers would torture the men and rape the women if given the opportunity. One can understand why many of them sadly committed suicide rather than fall into Allied hands.

After docking near the island, Sue and the other military personnel climbed over the rail of the ship and then down the side using rope ladders like the marines. They then boarded landing barges for transport ashore. Once on the beach, the group walked about 6 miles to a location where the hospital would be located. This would be unlike any other hospital Sue had worked in since it was only a series of tents; some for treating the injured men and others to house the medical staff. She had been trained to administer anesthesia during surgery and her responsibility here would be to serve as a nurse anesthetist. The hospital would be staffed by 24 surgeons and approximately 48 nurses.

At first, some of the doctors did not understand how dangerous Okinawa was. When a few of them left the hospital to go exploring, they were killed by Japanese.

Sue recalls, "We were taught that when traveling in a jeep to always have the women drive the men. If the men drove they would frequently be shot and any captured woman assaulted by the Japanese. Shooting the women was not worthwhile."

The surgeries took place in the tents. "I would often be providing anesthesia for up to three patients simultaneously," Sue admitted proudly. She mainly used ether but also sodium pentothal if it was available. Most of the serious injuries were men whose limbs had nearly been blown off by explosions. Some of them did not survive. Most did, however, and were either returned to their unit or sent for recuperation elsewhere after preliminary care.

The weather was usually sunny on Okinawa but there were many heavy rainstorms. "I vividly remember standing in my GI boots in mud up to my knees for some of the surgical procedures," Sue shared with a smile.

Morphine was available for pain relief. What was lacking, however, was the equipment to adequately sterilize surgical instruments. "But then this was not a hospital back in the states," Susan laughs.

Emergency care provided by the Navy corpsman in the field was so important for the wounded men. Many of them would not have lived if not for this initial medical care. While most of the patients undergoing surgery at their hospital had been wounded in Okinawa, some had been transferred from other islands such as the Marianas.

Attacks on the field hospital were rare but they did occur. Living through enemy bombing was very frightening. A few nurses lost their lives in this manner for there were few places to take cover.

A nearby city, Naha, had been nearly destroyed by Allied bombing so there wasn't much to do during lulls in the action. Sue remembers taking a ride with a young lieutenant, to whom she was nearly engaged, to an area where an Allied ship was docked. She was surprised to discover her brother there among the Navy personnel.

The food was not great on Okinawa. The troops lived on both C rations and K rations. The civilian population and Japanese troops had even less for sustenance.

On a few occasions, captured Japanese soldiers were brought to the hospital for treatment of their combat injuries. Sue remembers, "They were terrified and pleaded with the staff not to hurt them."

She thought it ironic for them to act this way. It was common knowledge that the Japanese had been brutalizing American soldiers throughout the Pacific.

After 82 consecutive days of battle, the hostilities finally ended on Okinawa but the loss of life was substantial. While the Allies had lost nearly 12,000, either killed or missing in action, the cost to the Japanese was much greater. It was estimated that between 70,000 and 130,000 Japanese died since many of their troops were incinerated in caves on the island. Civilian fatalities were even greater with many of them resulting from suicide rather than risk capture by the American soldiers.

While working on Okinawa, Sue began to have health problems of her own. She experienced very heavy menstrual bleeding and on one occasion even needed a transfusion. As a result of this, she developed hepatitis and was ill for many months.

One of her greatest experiences in the Pacific occurred on September 2, 1945, in Japan when she witnessed the Japanese surrender to General MacArthur while aboard the U.S.S. Missouri.

Sue was transferred to Korea where she continued to care for U.S. servicemen, but soon her medical condition worsened. She was shipped back to the United States to a hospital in Utica, New York, known as Rhodes Hospital, where she underwent surgery to remove her uterus.

After being discharged from the military Sue entered school at the University of Buffalo on the GI Bill. Here she obtained a bachelor's degree in nursing education. For the next few years she taught nursing at both the Millard Fillmore and Deaconess Hospital in Buffalo, New York. After completing the requirements for her masters in hospital administration, Sue became the director of nursing at Lafayette Hospital also in Buffalo.

Over the years she received her healthcare at Veterans Administration hospitals. Sue always felt that they were "very good to her." And it was at the VA Hospital in Canandaigua, New York, where I finally met this remarkable woman. For the last several years of her life I was her dentist. She wanted new teeth in the worst way. Sue was really having difficulty enjoying her favorite food, sweet corn.

On the day when Sue finally received her new teeth I also presented her with a plastic bag. It contained a little gift for her, three ears of fresh corn. I will always remember her giggling as she left the clinic that afternoon.

Sue Griffen as a young officer in the United States Army.

Sue Griffen during her time as our dental patient.

A TARGET OF OPPORTUNITY
-- DONALD BARTON

Donald Barton was the director of Cornell University's Experimental Station located at Geneva, New York, for over twenty two years. His Ph.D. in genetics prepared him for this challenging career and for the years following his retirement when he consulted in such countries as Pakistan, Indonesia, and India. He continues to thrive in his nineties enjoying fishing and traveling around the world. What few people realize is that his life before such a distinguished career in research may have even been more fascinating.

Donald grew up on a ranch near Fresno, California, and attended Berkeley College. In 1942, when the war began, he joined the Air Force Reserves in order to remain in college and have a choice once he was called up for duty. During his senior year, however, he was directed to report to the Preflight Orientation and Classification Center in Santa Anna, California. Here Don quickly learned that he would no longer be making his own decisions and that from then on would do everything on a schedule. Showering, using the bathroom, and having breakfast were now done with twenty other men.

Along with basic training, a series of tests were administered to determine which of these men were suitable to be members of an air crew. One could be selected for further training as a pilot, navigator, bombardier or member of a ground crew. Doing poorly on various tests such as the air chamber that simulated severe pressure changes resulted in one's "washing out" of the air cadets and any further training. After six weeks, he was successfully declared a cadet and sent to Roswell Air Base in New Mexico for training to become a bombardier.

The PX was the social center at the new base. Don recalls fondly the songs that played on the PX juke box during this period. Songs, such as "Blue Moon," "I Had the Craziest Dream" and "As Time Goes By," were drilled into his memory.

The course work at Roswell included studying aeronautics, navigation and the effects of speed and altitude on bomb trajectory. Here Don was introduced to the secret "Norden" bomb sight that was used for precision daylight bombing. This was basically a telescopic sight with a cushioned eyepiece. By adjusting several knobs one would be able to align the cross-hairs on the target. In the process, the bombsight would correct the plane's direction and determine precisely when to release the bombs. The pilot was responsible for maintaining altitude and speed during the "bomb run" while the bomb sight controlled the direction as the bombardier continued to make fine adjustments. A delicate touch was necessary and many men washed out here as a result of poor performance. Once Don completed this training, he was officially commissioned a second lieutenant/bombardier.

At Ephrata, Washington, Don joined a bomb group and trained with a crew for the next four weeks. Next he was sent to Rapid City, South Dakota, but after only two weeks was reassigned to Hutchinson, Kansas, for instruction as a navigator on a B-29 bomber. This was the largest four engine bomber used during the war and which was well suited for combat in the Pacific theater.

Now he had a dual rating qualifying him to fulfill both bombardier and navigator responsibilities in combat. After two months of training, pressurization problems in the B-29 were discovered that resulted in the windows blowing out. The huge B-29s were sent back to Wichita for corrections. Don was sent on to Alexandria, Louisiana, and reassigned to a new B-17 crew but his additional skill as a navigator would prove very useful later. His new crew proved to be a very focused and disciplined unit with better camaraderie than the previous crew.

Before shipping out, however, Don managed to have his college fiancé Virginia join him there and they were married on January 10, 1944. She would be his loyal companion for many happy years and help him to raise four wonderful children.

In Kearney, Nebraska, the crew picked up a brand new B-17 "Flying Fortress". After brief stops in New Hampshire, Goose Bay, Labrador, Reykjavik, Iceland, and Nutt's Corner, Ireland, they arrived in Peterborough, England. Because of the tremendous losses being sustained by the Eighth Air Force during that time, his crew immediately was assigned as a replacement to the 749th Bomb Squadron, 457th Bomb Group.

The first mission was to Nance, France, and since his plane was well back in the formation, he would only have to salvo his bombs when the lead plane with the bomb sight released its load. The target this day, a railroad marshalling yard, was heavily damaged. The return trip, however, did not go as well. Flak from a coastal antiaircraft battery tore through the Plexiglas and lacerated Don's hand. He would receive his first Purple Heart for this injury.

Several more combat missions followed including two that were to Berlin beyond the range of fighter escorts. On these missions he recalls the flak explosions being so heavy that there appeared to be black clouds over the city of Berlin.

Mission number 14, however, in late May of 1944, was expected to be a "milk run", one with lesser risk for antiaircraft or fighter resistance, but would prove to be one of his most significant. Twelve planes were assigned to bomb a V1 rocket installation in northern France near the Belgium border. Don's B-17 was to fly the lead, meaning he would have control of the bomb sight and determine when all of the planes would release their bomb loads. Unfortunately there was heavy cloud cover over the forest where the launch site was concealed so he could not be sure of hitting the target. On this particular mission, they were specifically directed not to bomb a target of opportunity. Knowledge of the proximity to the D-Day invasion a few days hence and the possibility of advance units in the region was unknown to most airmen at this time.

Don knew that that if he could not bomb this target that the mission would not count. Several of the twelve crews in the twelve plane group with him would be completing their required twenty-five missions and earning a trip home if they were successful. For that reason these men were assigned the milk run. He felt pressure to find and hit a target regardless of his preflight instructions regarding targets of opportunity. Returning without bombing the V1 site would mean these men would have to fly another mission in the future and possibly not survive.

In the distance, possibly twenty miles away, Don spotted an airfield near Lille, Belgium, and directed the pilot to fly towards this new target. The German airfield was "plastered" and no opposition was encountered. On the return flight back to England there were several very grateful and relieved crews. Colonel Luper, his commanding officer, was furious that Don had bombed this target of opportunity, a violation of direct orders. He was informed that he could expect further disciplinary action and possibly even court-martial. The twelve planes would not receive credit for a completed mission. After D-Day, however, Don was surprised to be reinstated as lead bombardier. He never heard another word about the expected discipline. The significance of the prior mission would not be known to him until much later.

At one a.m. on the 6th of June, 1944, Don's crew was called for a very early briefing and told that they were going to carpet bomb the area inland to the Normandy coast of France while allied troops were landing on the beachhead. This was different from previous missions where enemy fighters and antiaircraft hot spots could be expected. "Be sure not to bomb near the beaches," they were warned. As dawn was breaking, however, heavy cloud cover prevented his crew from witnessing the largest invasion force of any war in history.

On June 14, 1944, Don did not fly in "Bottoms Up" as his plane was called but was assigned as fill in for a crew whose navigator had recently been killed. The target would be the Le Bourget Airfield near Paris. He would be a member of the crew on the third plane of a twelve plane group. Not having worked as a navigator since his training, he did not have the maps listing the antiaircraft defensive positions from the intelligence rooms that the regular navigators had. His waist gunner, Gordon Long, was filling in also and was in Roy Allen's number two plane just ahead of his in the formation. His regular tail gunner was also included on the mission and flying in a plane further back in the formation.

Once they had reached the IP or initial point when the bomb run would begin, "all hell broke loose." The flak was everywhere and very accurate. Both the first and second planes were quickly shot down, but parachutes were evident as these planes fell from the sky. The third plane, the one Don was in, now became the lead. As navigator, Don would be responsible for guiding the group home safely. He carefully plotted his course back and made corrections when German antiaircraft batteries opened fire. He recalled that they always seemed to begin shooting while the planes were still out of range. The ten planes all returned with no further incident.

Some of the survivors from planes number one and two were not so lucky. Lieutenant Roy Allen and one hundred and sixty seven other allied airmen who had been aided by the French underground were arrested by the Gestapo while hiding in Paris. A traitor in the underground was responsible for their capture. All of the Allied airmen, or "Terror Fleigers" as they were called by the Germans that were captured during this raid, were unfortunately sent to Buchenwald concentration camp. Gordon was hidden by the partisans and actually worked for a time in a pub where the German soldiers drank. Once he had made his way back to the Allied lines just after the "break out" from St. Lo, France, the troops did not believe him. His identification papers and dog tags had been taken from him. Fortunately another soldier from his home town of Lexington, Kentucky, recognized him.

Several years ago, I had two veterans seated in my dental chairs await-ing treatment. One was Mr. Don Barton and the other was Mr. Richard Bedford. Before beginning Don's care, he told me about his drinking buddy, Roy Allen, from his bomb group who was shot down directly in front of him during a mission in World War II. This seemed ironic to me for the patient seated in my other chair was one of the airmen who had been sent to Buchenwald where he become friends with none other than the same Roy Allen.

Rouen, France, was the site of a large German fuel storage installation that became the target for their next mission on June 20, 1944. This would be a challenge for this depot was directly across the River Seine from the magnificent Rouen Cathedral. It was in Rouen, France, that St. Joan of Arc was burned at the stake centuries before the war. During the war the Allies attempted as much as possible not to destroy any structures with such his-toric significance nor injure civilians. Don was in the lead plane with the bomb sight and again would be the one who determined when all of the planes in the group released their bombs. They managed to hit the fuel depot precisely and spared the cathedral. For this precision bombing, he would later be awarded a letter of commendation from General Lacy.

The airmen had all heard rumors of a new technology recently devel-oped that would improve the accuracy when bombing through cloud cover. Don Barton discovered that he was one of five men selected from the Eighth Air Force to be trained to use this new "radar" for precision bombing. After being declared proficient, the crew was placed on alert to fly the next mission using radar. The ball turret of his plane, the pathfinder, or lead plane, had been replaced by a very conspicuous white dome. The predawn briefing identified the visual target for this thirty six plane wing to be a factory near Augsburg, Germany. If this was obscured by cloud cover then they were directed to bomb the city utilizing the radar. Only six members of his original crew would be on the lead plane for this trip. As it turned out the primary target was in fact hidden by clouds and as the group moved towards the secondary target, the formation was attacked by at least twelve Me109 fighter planes. Their lead plane took several hits from the 30 mm cannons on the initial pass resulting in the loss of one of their engines. After being knocked out of formation the attack continued on his lead plane. The decision was made to attempt to make it to Switzerland, a neutral country. Repeated attacks however seriously injured the navigator and disabled a second engine. "They continued to chew us up," is how Don described the attack. As the entire plane filled with smoke, the order was given to bail out.

Since the navigator had now lost consciousness a static cord was attached that would open his parachute and he was pushed out of the escape hatch. Don's crew had had only one simulated jump in training. He remembered that he should delay opening the chute until he could see ground below. Don had originally feared jumping out of a plane, but he knew that this was his only chance to survive.

Once out of the burning plane there was very little sensation of falling, only a sense of quiet, and calm, with a strong wind blowing from below. As soon as he could see the Tyrolean Alps below, he pulled his ripcord. He had been taught to flex his legs upon landing but unfortunately hit a boulder with his left leg and was seriously injured. Both bones were fractured and his ankle was dislocated. His foot now pointed backwards. Morphine in the escape kit provided some relief. While only twenty miles from Switzerland, Don was in no condition to walk down the mountain.

A couple of hours later, a teenage girl arrived wearing lederhosen. She said in perfect English. "I would like to help you out but I can't." Two German soldiers, and two Hitler Jugend (youth) arrived a while later. One of the youths was able to bandage his leg and, while Don was unconscious, they carried him down the mountain. A doctor arriving on the scene repositioned his ankle and splinted his leg.

A steam powered military truck was used to transport the new prisoner to Innsbruck and while on route they passed through several small villages. Don thought, "The attacks on the fuel depots must be taking a toll."

The truck stopped at an inn and one soldier went inside to get beer for the others. During this stop one member of the gathering crowd suggested that the airman be killed. This may have happened if not for the innkeeper who intervened. She said, "We would not want our boys treated this way." Soon the innkeeper's son came out and asked permission to take the prisoner inside to use the bathroom and have something to eat. He told Don that he was also a soldier but was on leave and that this region of Austria was sympathetic to the German cause. If he were in the hands of the right Austrians, they might have helped him get to Switzerland.

His name was Joseph Harting. Don gave him two British pennies that he had in his pocket and thanked the man for his kindness. Years after the war, Don returned to this very village and was fortunate to find the Austrian who had helped him that day.

Once Don arrived in Innsbruck, he was taken to a Luftwaffe hospital and then on to the university hospital for x-rays. Here another doctor who appeared very angry reset the broken leg. Later on at a hospital in Munich, a Luftwaffe doctor reset the leg properly at last and said that the prior physician had intentionally set it incorrectly. This military physician obviously adhered to the Geneva Convention.

Don remembers that, at the time, "Munich was a mess."

Frankfurt was the next stop, and the prisoner was placed in solitary confinement. The bed in his small 8 x 10 cell was infested with fleas and lice. Very little light entered the cell.

Don's interrogation then began. It consisted of three individuals seeking information for different reasons. The first, claiming to be from the Red

Cross, wanted information to relay to the U. S. and Don's family. The next interrogator, also an airman but of lesser rank, said that he was only doing his job. An officer of higher rank was last and he threatened to turn Don over to the Gestapo if he failed to cooperate. They already knew a considerable amount about the mission but wanted more information concerning the "new" technology utilized on his particular plane. They were unsuccessful with Don and got only name, rank and serial number.

The food he received consisted of potato soup with some cabbage and a single slice of black bread. While in solitary confinement, Don's body soon became covered with sores from the bites of the fleas and lice. There was one "moment of triumph" for Don in the stifling cell. He fabricated a sort of skate key from the metal tag on the heater with which he could unlock the small window for some fresh air.

Donald was next taken to the Frankfurt railroad yard and loaded onto a boxcar with other prisoners. The train departed after sunset to avoid attack from the Allied aircraft.

After arriving at the marshalling yard around noon on the following day, the air raid sirens began to wail. Through the small opening, three twelve plane groups of B-17s could be seen approaching. From his experience he knew that when the smoke flare from the lead plane was dropped that the bombs would detonate roughly two minutes later. Don recalls that this was one of his most terrifying moments during the war knowing that he could die at any moment and that there was absolutely nothing he could do about it. The irony of this statement is that he never really felt fear while flying combat missions. Fortunately his box car was spared.

After four days in transit the men arrived at their new home in Barth, Germany. The prison camp was located on a peninsula of land projecting into the Baltic Sea and intended to be escape proof. Five compounds each separated by barbed wire fencing were the home for nearly eight thousand Allied airmen and was known as Stalag Luft I.

Upon arrival, the men were allowed to shower. This was his first in several weeks. They were next treated with DDT powder to kill the fleas and lice covering their bodies. Don soon learned of an internal command chain established by the POWs. This was headed by Colonel Zemke and Lieutenant Colonel "Gabby" Gabraski, both of whom were fighter aces.

Conditions in the camp were tolerable at that time. Weekly showers were available and the meager food rations were supplemented with the weekly Red Cross parcels each man would receive. Each box contained powdered milk (klim), a chocolate bar, prunes, raisins, coffee, cheese, spam and cigarettes. These were sent from Sweden only sixty miles away. By the end of October, 1944, however, this luxury ceased. From that point until the end of the war the only food consisted of a bowl of rutabaga soup and a slice of black bread per day. One individual from each room was selected to divide the food evenly. The men would gather around making sure their ration was equal to the next. Ralph Mazydlo, a fireman from Milwaukie, was chosen in Don's particular room. Young men usually were preoccupied with thoughts of women and sex but when you are starving you become obsessed with food.

Each day several briquettes of coal were provided for each room. These were used for cooking and furnished the only warmth that was to be had in the uninsulated buildings during the cold winter. The men wore their clothes all the time and spent most of their time curled up on their straw beds trying to conserve warmth.

By the end of the war there were twenty four men crammed into the small room and it was difficult for the men not to irritate one another. Don remembers an African-American pilot named Sterling Penn from New York City. He was a great guy Don recalls. He was a member of the famed Tuskegee Airmen and had been flying out of Italy until captured. Rooming with him and several boys from the south proved to be interesting during their stay at Stalag Luft I.

Items such as cigarettes from the Red Cross parcels were often traded with these older German guards who were otherwise unfit for duty. With materials acquired from outside the camp the men were able to build a crystal radio receiver. Daily BBC broadcasts could be monitored and the news shared among the prisoners. This proved to be very important to maintain the morale in the prison camp. This radio was disassembled and the parts hidden each time the German guards who knew of its existence came to search the rooms.

With time it became apparent to the guards that the end of the war was imminent and the military discipline softened. The real question became who would actually liberate the prisoners: the Allied troops from the west or the Russians from the east. Once the German commandant in charge realized that the Russians would arrive first, he attempted to surrender to Colonel Zemke, the POW leader, in order to protect his men. Zemke refused and suggested that the Germans simply leave. All of the prisoners recall the announcement over the camp's PA system notifying the men that the U.S. and British officers were now in control of the camp. Zemke said. "I am now in control of the camp, the Germans have left." It was May 1, 1945.

Some of the prisoners who could speak Russian were sent out to meet the advancing units and informed the Russians of the existence of the prison camp nearby. The prisoners were then allowed to leave the camp and secure food from the farms nearby. The German people were treated brutally by the Russians who recalled their treatment during the German invasion early in the war. On May the eighth, the prisoners were notified that Hitler was dead and that Germany had surrendered.

On May 16th the Allied prisoners were thrilled to hear American B-17s and B-24s arriving to begin their evacuation from Barth. Several hundred planes successfully airlifted nearly eight thousand Allied prisoners in only 48 hours. Don recalls the exhilaration he felt when his plane was airborne and he was finally free.

The men were in very poor physical condition when they arrived in Rheims, France, with Don weighing only 116 pounds. They were advised to eat very carefully to regain their strength. Don boarded a hospital train for Le Havre and stopped briefly at Rouen. As you will recall it was here that Don's plane had led a group of twelve B-17s months earlier. Now he actually was standing in front of the Rouen Cathedral across the river from the site of the now destroyed German fuel depot.

On the same date of that highly successful mission some fifty four years later, his cousin would visit this very place while on a tour up the Seine River with other Stanford University alumni. Here reports detailing the mission by a Lieutenant Barton were read to the tour group by the boat's captain. While this incident may seem amazing to many the following story may surprise the reader even more so.

Many people recall the well-known movie, "The Longest Day", about the Normandy invasion marking the turning point in World War II. During a segment of the movie two German fighter planes strafed the beaches but inflicted little damage to the Allied forces storming the beachhead. Interviews of German Luftwaffe officers after the war's end revealed that about ninety planes of the forward element of the German fighter wing had been at Lille, Belgium, prior to the D-Day invasion. This base was about 180 miles from the site of the invasion. A heavy bombing attack a week before the invasion destroyed many of these aircraft. The surviving planes were then moved south to Nance, France, about 90 miles further away and now out of range of the Normandy beachhead. Only two planes were left behind and these were the only available to help repel the Allied forces. Would this landing of the largest invasion force in the history of war have been different if Lieutenant Barton's mission, for which credit was never given, had not destroyed that airfield at Lille, Belgium? One can only speculate as to what may have transpired on that historic day June 6, 1944.

Recently, Mr. Barton was one of several veterans invited to speak at a World War II remembrance ceremony in Rochester, New York. He shared the story of the mission that he led with an audience of nearly two hundred guests. I recall wondering at the time if most of them really realized the significance of his "failed mission".

Near the end of the evening there was a "sing along" where we all sang songs that were popular during the war. When asked if there were any other songs that members of the audience wished to sing, Don slowly stood up. He stated that he did know one but that he would have to sing it alone. For while most may know the melody, we certainly would not know the lyrics. And then he proceeded to sing to the tune of "As Time Goes By"…

> It's still the same old story
> The colonels get the glory
> On that you can rely
> You know the odds are too darn high
> As flak goes by
> One tens and two tens coming at 800
> Turn on the bomb sight got to kill the rate
> If they don't go salvo don't wait
> The target's rushing by
> It's still the same old story
> The colonel's get the glory
> On that you can rely
> You know the odds are too darn high
> As flak goes by…..

Left: Smiling young airman early in the war. Below: the Norden bombsight.

Don reunited with Innkeeper's son in Austria.

Don Barton during an interview

PARTISANS --ALBERT PISTILLI

Albert Pistilli was not only one of my patients, but the grand-father of one on my son's close friends during high school. While his experiences in combat during World War II are significant, what occurred after capture and subsequent escape make his story in Al's words, "almost unbelievable".

Born in Rochester, New York, Al enjoyed a normal upbringing until he was drafted in 1943. After completing thirteen weeks of basic training at Fort McClellan in Alabama, Al traveled to Camp Rucker, also in Alabama, where he practiced military drills such as landings and ground assaults.

Eventually, he was shipped to North Africa and then to Italy as part of the 45th Infantry Division. The 45th saw action at Salerno, Italy and by Christmas 1943, the division was sent north to Mt. Casino where the Americans were bogged down under the relentless barrage of huge German guns that were mounted on railroad tracks. These were retracted into the mountains after firing their deadly loads of explosives.

Their next Italian objective was Anzio. Two battalions of the 45th Division along with forces from Canada, New Zealand, and England encountered little resistance. This was fine for Al for he was part of the first wave to land on the beaches. After making some progress, the men were forced to withdraw due to supply shortages. This provided a perfect opportunity for the German forces to counterattack. Soon the Allies were pinned down on the beachhead. After nearly one month of heavy combat with terrible losses, the Allied forces began a second assault inland. By this time his company of 179 men had needed 211 replacements since so many men had been killed or wounded. Al still does not know how he managed to live through this.

"Somebody upstairs was watching out for me," were the words he used to describe his surviving the savage battle.

One evening, he was ordered to set up his mortar and commence firing as soon as they could begin to hear their Allied tanks approaching from behind. The smoke screen used for protection began to clear and soon he could hear the tanks. They were not behind but directly in front of his foxhole. The next thing he could see was the huge 88 mm cannon on the German tank crest the hill and point directly at them. There was nothing they could do to defend themselves and they prepared to die. The tank did not fire. Four German soldiers climbed out of the tank and demanded that they surrender. The entire squad was captured, strip searched and marched away to begin their ordeal as prisoners of war.

It had been cold up to this point and now snow began to fall. None of the nearly thirty captured men knew what to expect next and discovered that all would be interrogated after a brief march. The German officer in charge began his questioning by informing the prisoners in perfect English that he also was an American citizen. They were all shocked. "I am from Philadelphia but left the U.S. after the war began to join the better team," he proudly stated.

The prisoners began to realize that they were more valuable to the enemy alive for bargaining purposes and possible sources of information. "All we would say was our name, rank, and serial number," Al recalls.

The forced march that followed was grueling and long. They were hungry, cold and tired. Any man who fell behind was simply shot. The compound they were led to was located in what was known as Cina Cita. The facility was a casting studio for movie production. One thousand men were held in a single building containing no bathroom facilities and surrounded by layers of barbed wire.

Food was scarce for the prisoners as well as for the enemy soldiers. Al remembers, "One large cauldron filled with water, some vegetables, and various animal parts, including a cow's head, was boiled to produce a broth. This was served in our helmets along with a small portion of black bread. A loaf was given to every seventh prisoner to divide amongst the other six."

The men were allowed to go outside the building during daytime. After a while they were allowed to dig a trench outside near the barrier that could serve as a latrine. This was an improvement over using the floor of the building where they slept.

After nearly two weeks in captivity, Al was joined by a young man he had trained with back in the States named Jack O'Neil. He was from New Jersey. Jack saw Al and asked. "How are the conditions here?"

"Terrible," Al responded.

"What are we doing here?" Jack said next.

"If you have an idea, I'm with you," answered Al.

Nearby was a railroad that was the object of daily bombing they discovered. The prisoners were expected to repair this damage afterwards. During these attacks the men would be herded inside as the guards begin firing from the antiaircraft batteries at the attacking Allied planes.

Jack was the one who noted the regularity of the bombing. It occurred daily at around 10 a.m. They devised a plan to escape during the next attack. The stakes were high. Failure would mean certain death. If they could dive into the latrine during the next Allied bombing and crawl to the fence they might be able to escape.

Their opportunity arrived the next day and they dove into the foul trench filled with urine and feces. As they crawled towards the barbed wire they discovered another man waiting.

"Are you coming? "Al shouted.

"No," was his reply.

"Hold up the G...D...barbed wire!" Al demanded.

The other prisoner held the fence apart for them to escape. They ran about 600 yards to the next building that they realized held sets for the movies produced there.

When darkness arrived they made their way to freedom. There was only one problem now. Which way to proceed?

As luck would have it, Al noticed a structure in the distance at daybreak. It looked strangely familiar. Could it really be the aqueduct he had studied in school as a boy? If he was correct this would lead directly to Rome. Jack and he hid during the day and slowly made their way, under the cover of darkness, towards Rome via the aqueduct and, they hoped to freedom.

The plan was to hide during the daytime and move under the cover of darkness. Although they were not followed their next critical problem was finding food. After four days with nothing to eat, they were starving.

Al thought as he looked at the road nearby, "The next guy who comes by, I'm stopping." This was a huge risk. He could speak some Italian and hoped that whoever it was would not turn them over to the Germans. Al jumped out in front of a man and began to speak in Italian. This man's face broke into a broad smile and said, "Come with me."

Jack and Al were taken to a farm where they were given some food and clothing. They were instructed to spend the days out in the field working, picking vegetables and weeding.

"How could we have been so lucky?" Al remembers. After a week Jack and "Alberto," as he was now called, boarded a donkey drawn cart destined to deliver produce to the Vatican. They were warned, "Do not say a thing."

In those days Rome was considered to be an "open city" but still under control of the German Gestapo. At the Vatican, they were greeted by a monsignor originally from Detroit who had been trapped in Rome since the start of the war. He told them of plans to assist the two men. In the meantime, they received new civilian clothes and were instructed to stay in the Vatican.

While living there, Al was introduced to a Brother who was studying at the Vatican and attempting to learn to speak English. After two weeks spending virtually all of his time with Brother Dom, it was decided that Al would speak only Italian and Dom only English. Soon they both became proficient in these languages.

Al slept in the catacombs of St. Callistus while Brother Dom went to classes during the day. One night Dom came to Al and asked him to accompany him as he climbed to one of the hilltops nearby. Al was instructed to "keep your eyes open." In a few minutes a train appeared in the distance and as Al watched, there was a sudden explosion. The train was destroyed. The partisans were at work!

The next day, in retaliation for the bombing of the train, the Germans rounded up 120 civilians and executed them outside of Rome. The story was actually written up in "Life" magazine shortly after this happened.

A few weeks later "Alberto" was told that there was an assignment for the men. They were instructed to follow two men traveling by streetcar. They arrived at their destination, #20 Via Empiria, Rome, where they would reside in the home of the wife of the ambassador from Malta to Italy. Her husband had recently passed away but she remained in Rome with her five daughters and son because of the war.

Al and Jack were given money and instructed to spend their hours mingling with the Italian citizens in an attempt to locate other escaped Allied soldiers. The prison camps in North Africa had dispersed and many of the Allied officers from there were making their way up through Italy in an attempt to rejoin the Allied forces. Once found, they could be repatriated. Jack and Al soon found that the bars were the best places to hunt but they had to be very careful. Jack was advised to let Al do the talking. Jack had blond hair and actually fit in well in Rome.

Al recalls having a fake passport and papers stating that he was a German antiaircraft gunner on leave. Once contact was established with soldiers wishing to reach Allied lines, arrangements would be made to repatriate them. This was commonly done under the cover of darkness in one of two ways. They were either taken to fields where piper cub planes could evacuate them or delivered to rowboats on the beach for transport out to waiting submarines. This was their assignment from February to May of 1944.

One particular officer from New Zealand was hiding in a hotel and a plan had been made to assist in his escape. Unfortunately, the Germans discovered his whereabouts and moved in to arrest him. Al and Jack somehow found a way out of the hotel. The officer was hiding in a room occupied by a woman so he tried to disguise himself by using her clothing. This did not work. The man of well over six feet was being dragged from the building by two much smaller German soldiers. Once he realized that he was so much bigger he turned and knocked both Germans to the ground and escaped. Al laughs to this day as he remembers the fellow from New Zealand running away wearing high heels!

The ambassador's wife was a remarkable woman. She had recently donated all of the gold at the embassy to Mussolini in support of the Fascists. Her picture had been in all of the papers doing so but in reality she was supporting the Allied effort.

Al Pistilli recounted to me the following story one day while he sat in my dental chair. This is when I concluded that his military experiences were truly unique.

When Field Marshall Kesselring arrived in Rome to inspect the troops, arrangements were made for him and his entourage to see "Madame Butterfly" at the Rome Opera House.

"On the day of the opera, a courier arrived with two tickets for the ambassador's wife Gracia and one of her daughters to attend. They were considered honored guests."

"Unfortunately, the ambassador's wife was ill and she asked Alberto, as I was now called, to take her daughter Gema to the performance. The theater was alive with excitement and all of the honored guests including the daughter Gema and me were taken to their seats. I was luckily seated at the end of the aisle so I would not have to speak to anyone. We were in the second row with the front row empty."

"Herr Field Marshal and his staff walked into the opera house with everyone shouting "Sieg Heil" and standing at attention. They proceeded to the same aisle we were seated in. Their seats were next to Gema's. I got up to let them in and Field Marshal Kesselring sat for the entire opera on the other side of Gema. Who would have thought that an escaped Allied prisoner could sit so close to one of the highest ranking German officers and remain undetected?"

Al remembers a very interesting portion of this opera.

"A certain character, Lt. Pickering, would regularly visit a Japanese lady and bring her a box of goodies. The box contained a carton of Lucky Strike cigarettes. At the time, I was smoking like a fiend but had not had an American cigarette in months."

These tickets were Al's souvenirs of this terrifying experience and he kept them for many years. Unfortunately, years after the war, one of his children took them to school for "show and tell" while the class studied the war. She never brought the tickets home.

As the war progressed so did the Allied movement northward in Italy. It was June 6th, 1944, when the Allied troops moved into Rome. Knowing that the enemy was advancing, the Germans had placed explosives on many bridges that would need to be crossed. The partisans sent Al and Jack to the Tiber River to clear the bridge. While doing so the first American tank arrived and quickly discovered that these two Italian citizens were in fact escaped Allied soldiers. Once found they were quickly returned to the Fifth Army headquarters for debriefing and a meeting with General Mark Clark. After explaining all that had transpired both Jack and Al were sent to Washington for more debriefing at the Pentagon. After nearly two weeks of questioning, they were told not to tell anyone what they had experienced. Other Allied personnel were working behind enemy lines and their lives would be in jeopardy if any of this information was disclosed. News of these returning soldiers eventually reached the media and Al was offered twenty thousand dollars for the story by Coronet magazine, a popular publication at the time. As loyal soldiers, they both declined.

Al was given a forty five day leave from the army to return home to Rochester, but unfortunately had no money. There were many scams operating at this time with people seeking money from families of soldiers who were listed as "missing in action". When Al borrowed money to send a telegram to his father asking for money to come home, his dad refused, believing that his son was dead. Luckily his girlfriend and mother convinced his father to wire the twenty five dollars for a train home. When he finally arrived home there were sixty relatives waiting to see this "dead soldier come back to life."

While on furlough, Al was married to his sweetheart Cathy. In those days, people gave you money instead of presents when you got married. Al had also just received six months back pay for the period since he was captured so he and his bride were flush with cash.

Since he was still technically in the army, they were sent to a base near Durham, North Carolina. Here they were allowed to live off the base in a motel. They met four other men who had also just returned to the United States, who also had a lot of money. Cathy would actually find dates for the other men and they would party. They actually hired a taxi to stay at the motel 24 hours a day for transportation to get to town.

The four men and Al were reassigned to Camp Croft, North Carolina, where their commanding officer had a unique idea how to use these "combat veterans". He felt that for the entire 13 weeks of basic training, the recruits never really experienced actual combat experience with "live fire". He ordered Al and the other four men to devise a training plan to expose one squad at a time to this "realistic experience". While on a scouting mission the squad would come under live machine gun fire from Al and the others, and have to devise a plan to neutralize the "enemy". They were very successful and their Commanding Officer decided to add a 14th week to the basic training that would include this.

Now Al and the others were really living like kings with their own personal jeeps and plenty of money to spend in Spartanburg. That is, until the colonel called Al into his office.

"How would you like to get out of the army?" he asked smiling.

Al replied, "Yes."

"According to the Geneva Convention, any man who was unattached and behind enemy lines for more than thirty days is eligible for immediate discharge," the colonel informed him. Al was discharged three days later while the war was still on.

He and Cathy returned to Rochester where he had a successful career as a businessman, and their family eventually grew to include 6 children. It was Al's suggestion that the stories he and other veterans have told me should be saved and shared. When I recorded his interview he said, "Much of what I am telling you must seem unbelievable but it actually happened."

I do believe him and he is correct. This is probably the most unbelievable story I have ever heard from any combat veteran.

Young Al with his friend Jack O'Neil

Al dressed as a civilian during the war in Italy.

Al on the left with three of the daughters and some of the partisans. The man in the middle is an escaped British officer.

Gema, the daughter who accompanied Al to the opera.

The day Al was liberated by the two GI's on the left, June 6. 1944.

Al Pistilli more recently.

A BUDDY -- RALPH FELICE

A youngster from Geneva, New York, needed to write a paper for school and after some thought decided he would tell the story of his hero, his grandfather Ralph, and a man he served with, Joseph Guigino, during World War II. The story of the two best friends would soon reach far beyond the high school he attended and recognize these two veterans who sacrificed so much for their country.

I first met his grandfather as my patient several years ago but he rarely spoke of the war. Ralph always had a smile on his face and was very proud of his family. He worked as an electrician and spent his spare time tending his vast vegetable garden. It was always a special day when he arrived for his appointment with me with a huge load of garlic.

He greeted me with, "Here, Doc. These are for you."

The staff always shared the garlic. They were probably the largest and most flavorful I have ever tasted.

He also shared with me his technical expertise. When I encountered an electrical problem at home, he usually had the solution.

One December day, Ralph sat in my chair and said somberly, "Today is my anniversary- the day I was captured. I remember the snow was nearly up to my waist. I will never forget that day."

Ralph Felice was born August 28, 1925, and along with five siblings, grew up in the city of Geneva, New York, on the north end of Seneca Lake. While in high school, he quickly learned about the war and was assigned a project that could possibly help defend his homeland. He was asked to build models of American planes that could be used by civil defense workers stationed in air field towers. Any aircraft observed for which there was not a corresponding model would be considered an attacking enemy plane and immediately reported. He was very proud of this project and a picture of Ralph along with his models appeared in the local newspaper.

He graduated in June of 1943, and in October was drafted into the United States Army. Ralph remembers driving his brother, Tony, to the Lehigh Valley Railroad station to report for duty. Later that same day, he delivered his other brother, Freddie, to the New York Central Railroad station for the same purpose. The two brothers would arrive back home years later and be picked up by Ralph on the same day. A third brother also served during the war. All of the young servicemen were treated well by the civilian population Ralph recalls. On his furlough after basic training, a friend who had been disabled at Pearl Harbor loaned Ralph his new Buick to use during his time home. Any green ration stamps he used to purchase gas at the local gas station were returned to Ralph by the station's owner so he could give them to his father who put them to good use during this time of strict rationing.

The next ten months were spent in Mississippi where Ralph trained as part of an antitank battalion and member of the106th Infantry Division along with 15,000 other men. Here he met a lad who would become his best friend, Joe Guigino, from Massachusetts. Once this training was completed they were surprisingly sent to Massachusetts in preparation for their journey overseas. For the next two weeks they were so close to Joe's home that they spent all their free time there roller skating, playing the player piano, and fooling around. Ralph became part of Joe's family and was treated like another son. The enjoyment ended when they crossed the Atlantic to England and finally arrived in Le Havre, France. As a Private First Class Ralph was now earning $24 a month which was good money after growing up in the depression.

The 106th Division moved quickly through France and then made its way to the border between Belgium and Germany. The Siegfried line here was a barrier that had been constructed to prevent invasion of Germany by enemy armor. The metal reinforced concrete posts were spaced in such a way to prevent entry and were supported by concrete pillboxes. Soon intense fighting began and by the third day two of his friends, one from New York City and one from New Jersey, were dead.

Ralph was selected to become the company runner replacing his buddy "Tiny", the previous runner, who had also been quickly killed. His job was to relay messages day and night, sometimes running 2 to 3 miles at a time through the combat zone.

His next job was to drive a truck that pulled a 105 mm Howitzer artillery piece. The men were in the Hürtgen Forest region of Germany and preparing for an anticipated German counter offensive later known as the Battle of the Bulge.

On the 16th of December 1944, a ferocious blizzard hit. It was cold and the snow became very deep. Luckily, they had been issued some cold weather clothing including a heavy overcoat, but their footwear was inadequate. The 423rd Regiment was moving slowly through a valley when enemy soldiers on both sides opened up. For three horrible days the battle continued and they were losing "a lot of men". In addition to dealing with the attacking Germans, the Americans were also suffering from frozen feet. They could not hold out much longer and began to prepare for surrender by breaking their guns against nearby trees so that they could not be used by the enemy. Nearly one third of the Regiment had already been killed by this time.

The battle was finally over on December 19th and the surviving men were herded together as prisoners of war of the Third Reich. They began their slow march several miles into Germany. All the men were exhausted with many injured from their horrible ordeal. Personal property of any value as well as their overcoats were soon confiscated by their captors.

Ralph's wristwatch, pen, and high school ring were taken from him. They continued their journey on 40x8 boxcars until the train was attacked by RAF planes. When the doors were blown off of their boxcar, Ralph and Joe jumped out to escape but soon broke through the ice of a pond they attempted to cross and were quickly caught.

They arrived at their new destination at 4 p.m. on Christmas Day. Their new home was known as Stalag 9b where they slept on lice infested straw piled on the floor. A small stove located in the center of the barracks provided little if any heat.

Ralph's parents were distraught when they were notified that their son Freddie had been wounded in combat. A second telegraph soon arrived stating that another son, Ralph, was missing in action. This was nearly more than they could bear. The comfort provided by neighbors, friends and the parish priest was something Ralph will be forever thankful for.

One day the German guards distributed cards for the prisoners to fill out stating that these would be sent to their families back home. The prisoners really did not believe that this would ever happen. Ralph's parents eventually did receive the card stating that their son was now a prisoner of war. It was the second week of February, 1945.

When Allied planes bombed the nearby railroad, which seemed to happen daily, the prisoners were forced to repair the damage. The men had to cut grooves in logs to replace the damaged railroad ties. The rails were attached with spikes found buried in the deep snow after these attacks. During this time of forced labor, their food consisted of a few potatoes and some broth. With time all the prisoners began to lose weight.

Sounds of combat in the distance began to reach the imprisoned men as time went on. Ralph remembers an Allied fighter plane chasing an enemy Me109 over the prison camp. While he downed the enemy plane, the pilot had inadvertently hit several of the prisoners. Ralph remembers that Joe Schmidt, an 80-year-old guard, treated the prisoners decently. He told the prisoners he had kids in the service and this affected the way he treated these American boys. While Red Cross parcels containing food were distributed to other Allied prison camps, Ralph only received one. The men surmised that the Germans must have been keeping them since their food reserves were very low.

On April 2, 1945, Ralph's mother's birthday, General Patton's tanks crashed through the gates of their compound. These malnourished men were now free. When Ralph had entered the service he weighed 142 pounds. He now only weighed 84 pounds. A Captain suggested that they make Joe Schmidt the guard their prisoner but the men instead drove him to a nearby town where he resided. They considered him a "nice guy" in spite of him being the enemy.

The newly freed men were sent back to France where they were finally deloused by American medics. This infestation is something all prisoners remember vividly. "The lice would get into your skin and the men were afraid to scratch for fear of getting an infection," Ralph admitted.

The men were advised not to overeat in spite of their hunger. Real milk and white bread was about all Ralph could tolerate at this time. He returned to the United States and was initially sent to Lake Placid to recover from this ordeal. Clean sheets and clean dishes were almost too good to be true. On May 8, 1945, he participated in a parade in his hometown of Geneva, New York.

Ralph recalls, "When I left for the service my mother had dark black hair, but it had become pure white by the time her sons returned home."

Ralph was scheduled to be discharged but became ill with hepatitis. He was sent to a hospital in Boston, Massachusetts, to recover. While there, he decided to contact the family of his best friend Joe and find out where he was. Joe's parents said that he was also in a hospital in Boston recovering. It was the same hospital Ralph was in. Ralph asked the nurses to tell Joe, his buddy, that Ralph was in the same hospital. Even though he was in poor condition, Joe, upon discovering this, insisted that his bed be taken to where Ralph was.

After the war Ralph and his wife raised two daughters and had several grandchildren. In the years that followed Ralph's and Joe's families continued to visit one another and the two men remained close friends until Joe passed away a few years ago. That was when Ralph's grandson, Cameron, was inspired to write the story of his "hero" Ralph and best friend Joe. The report was so well written that Ralph had a copy sent to Joseph's son, a policeman in Boston. He was so moved by this article that he forwarded it to the Chamber of Commerce for consideration. After reviewing the document and doing some additional research the decision was made to recognize their hometown hero in some special way.

In 2006 Ralph Felice and his family travelled to Boston to attend the ceremony and dedication of what is now known as "Joe Guigino Boulevard" in honor of his "best friend".

This past fall, I was asked to be the keynote speaker for the annual MIA/POW recognition day. Having recently returned from visiting the beaches of Normandy provided much inspiration for me. I was privileged to see many of my former patients/friends there including Ralph and his grandson, Cameron.

Ralph smiled and said proudly, "Doc, I want you to meet my grandson, Cameron."

"Can I take a picture of you with my Grandpa?" Cameron requested.

"Sure! But only if I can have a copy," I eagerly replied. As I got up to leave his table the thought occurred to me that I had not had any of the special garlic since I retired.

"Do you still grow the garlic Mr. Felice?" I asked having been raised to respect my elders.

"Absolutely!" Ralph replied. "I will bring you some next summer."

Ralph Felice once told me that he had had a lot of thrills in his life. The biggest thrill, however, occurred when the ship, on which he returned home to the United States, made a special trip to the Statue of Liberty.

How many Americans today would be moved in such a manner as Ralph was nearly seventy years ago?

Young Ralph (right) working with his models during high school.

Ralph on furlough with the Buick.

Young Ralph in his dress uniform

Ralph with Doc at the MIA/POW reunion.

THE GAMBLER -- BOB BAKER

Both Bob and his navigator enjoyed playing bridge and with the cards they discovered in their Red Cross parcels, they proceeded to teach the other men in the barracks how to play the game. By the time they were released from the prisons of the Third Reich, they had all become experts.

Bob Baker had been raised in the 19th Ward of Rochester, New York, and, like most other boys, really enjoyed playing baseball. After graduating from West High School, his plans for the future were soon altered by the attack on Pearl Harbor. Young men at this time were eager to go to the defense of their country, but Bob really wanted no part of the infantry so he enlisted in the Army Air Corps in February of 1942. His intention was to become a pilot, so he was sent to Texas to begin cadet training. Once there, however, his depth perception was determined to be poor so he was instead transferred to bombardier school. Bob would later laugh at this fact since the dexterity and control necessary as a bombardier was as great as what was needed to fly a plane.

His first experience in a plane during a severe storm made him very sick, but with time Bob adjusted to the changes one felt flying in a plane. After nearly eight months of training at both Ellis Air Base in Houston and Big Spring, Texas, he graduated from the program. It was June of 1943, when he graduated from bombardier school and received his wings as a second lieutenant. His parents and girlfriend, Charlotte, traveled all the way from Rochester to attend this event. Bob was granted a 10 day leave so he returned home with his family and while there proposed to Charlotte.

With only three days to plan the wedding, they still succeeded in filling St. Stephen's Church for the special occasion. Their honeymoon was only two nights at the Hilton Hotel in Buffalo, New York.

After one month at gunnery school in Laredo, Texas, it was off to Moses Lake, Washington. Bob was happy to finally be away from all the flat land he had seen in Texas but, unfortunately, it was more of the same at the new base. Weeks of training followed and soon the men were assigned to a crew of the "Flying Fortress", the B-17. The men trained together as a team for the next four months and flew many practice missions. Bob was expected to hit targets with small bombs and become proficient with the Norden bomb site. Using this piece of new technology allowed for more precision when bombing enemy targets.

Bob and his crew were sent for the next three months to a base in Rapid City, South Dakota, for additional training. Since the bombardier was expected to manage one of the 50 caliber machine guns in the heavy bomber, Bob received more training with this weapon. During his down time there, Bob enjoyed hunting pheasants that were plentiful in this part of the country. All his gunnery training had made him an excellent shot.

The crew was now ready for combat and they were flown to New York City in December, 1943. After spending the night there, the men departed for Goose Bay, Labrador. His crew was split up for this trip and rode in two B-17s, with the planes being flown by pilots, copilots and navigators from air transport command. These three men had obviously not had that much experience with the B-17 and what happened during the last leg of the journey to England was a terrifying experience for everyone on board. The weather was terrible so the pilot of Bob's plane climbed to nearly 32,000 feet for improved visibility. Bob and the other men in the rear noticed that they were getting lightheaded and Bob went up to the cockpit to investigate. The three air transport men were wearing their oxygen masks but had failed to tell their passengers to do the same.

This first crisis was followed by a second when the wings of their plane iced up causing the plane to become difficult to control. A steady descent followed with the inexperienced pilot becoming very alarmed. He finally called in the terrifying words, "Mayday – Mayday". They might not make it. The passengers, the new B-17 crew, were terrified knowing that they could not bail out over the Atlantic Ocean in December. Just when they thought their time was up, the plane broke out of the clouds. The ordeal was over! Upon landing in Nutt's Corners, Ireland, Bob and his crew knelt down to kiss the ground they thought they would never touch again. It was discovered that the plane had only enough gas left in the tanks for ten more minutes in the air. Bob said that this experience was nearly as scary as his worst combat mission.

Bob Baker and his crew were assigned to the 381st Bomb Group in Ridgewell, England, their home for the next few months. Now they would be flying in "real" combat missions where they would be in terrible danger. They would be targets for the German Luftwaffe and antiaircraft batteries. On the day of a mission, the men were awakened at 3:00 a.m. for breakfast of powdered eggs and coffee followed by the very important briefing. There, the target for the day's mission would be disclosed. Often groans would greet the officers conducting the briefing when the crews learned of the more dangerous targets. The heavy bombers were loaded with bombs and ammunition and were ready to depart by six in the morning. Lifting off with such a heavy load of explosives was the first of many challenges on such a day.

Planes from many other bases scattered over the English countryside would then rendezvous over the next hour or more and begin their journey over Nazi occupied Europe. On the earlier missions, P-47 Thunderbolts would be their escort providing protection for the slower heavy bombers. Later when the targets were deeper into Germany, the longer range of the P-51 Mustangs was necessary. Enemy fighter planes and exploding flak were a real threat for all of their missions. For some of them, hundreds of aircraft would be involved. The bombers flew in tight formations to maximize their defensive potential. With each of the planes possessing 10-50 caliber machine guns, the bombers would mean a dangerous target for the attacking Luftwaffe. During most of the journey, Bob was required to man one of these guns in the nose of the plane. His protection here was only the Plexiglas and a flak vest that he did not wear. Instead, he sat on the vest believing it more important to protect his "bottom."

Once near the target, however, he took control of the plane during the final approach by making fine adjustments to the Norden bomb site. The Norden could calculate the exact point for release of their bombs so as to inflict maximum damage on the target. The pilot's responsibility was to maintain speed and altitude as the target was approached. Once Bob could see it in the crosshairs, he would say, "Give me control of the plane." He could actually move the plane right or left with the bomb sight. Once the bombs were released, the pilot again took control of the B-17.

On the days when there were no missions to be flown the men were able to relax. They would often get bikes and take a ride through the English countryside. The local residents would often give them food like "real" eggs to cook which was a special treat for these airmen.

An airman was allowed to return to the United States if he successfully completed 25 missions, but the likelihood of this happening was remote. At that time, the losses sustained by the Eighth Air Force were significant. If you were not wounded or killed, being captured was a very real possibility. Bob would never complete the required number of missions and was nearly shot down on his fifth mission to Augsburg, Germany. His B-17 was riddled with holes and limped back to England with only three of the four engines functioning. The crews were always relieved when the White Cliffs of Dover came into view.

The briefing for the seventh mission on March 6, 1944, was one Bob would never forget. The target would be the heart of the Third Reich, Berlin, and the first time that city was attacked by the Allies. Nearly 1200 heavy bombers, both B-17s and B-24s, were scheduled to fly. The German defenses surrounding Berlin were formidable. In addition to the enemy antiaircraft filling the skies with exploding flak, hundreds of fighter planes attacked the formations of Allied bombers. It was such a clear day and both JU88s and Me109s could be seen attacking from all directions. The Germans were "throwing everything they had" at the bombers to protect Berlin.

"We were scared to death," Bob recalls.

By the time his plane reached Magdeburg, nearly 50 miles from the target in Berlin, they were already under heavy attack. The records will show that 64 B-17s were lost, but the cost to the enemy was even higher with 164 of their planes shot down during that horrific battle. Bob's plane was hit numerous times and before long, two engines were ablaze. The section of the plane containing the tail gunner was blown completely off of the bomber. Soon his burning plane fell out of formation. The order was given to "bail out". Before Bob could leave, he needed to open the bomb bay doors and release the bombs. The crew members in the rear of the plane could then escape. Bob, the navigator, pilot and copilot then went out the front hatch. The radioman, waist gunners, top, and ball turret gunners also escaped. Miraculously nine of the 10 men had survived. Witnesses in nearby planes stated that Bob's plane exploded shortly after the men bailed out.

These men had been taught how to deploy the chest pack parachute but had been advised to do so only after they had fallen to at least 10,000 feet. This was because of the lack of oxygen at higher altitudes. Also, they would not present easy targets for the enemy below during the freefall. How was he to know when he fell this far? He succeeded in opening the parachute he estimates at about 8,000 feet and floated down into a tree. After finding himself suspended nearly 20 feet above the ground, Bob eventually released the harness and fell to the ground. In doing so, he seriously hurt his back, an injury that would bother him for many years following the war.

Within three hours all of his crew had been captured and taken to a jail in a nearby village. Luckily, Bob had thrown his hand gun away before bailing out or he probably would have been shot. Along the way the civilians would shout at them and pelt them with objects. The airmen were next moved to Dulog Luft in Frankfurt for interrogation. In spite of the threats received such as, "You may get killed if you don't talk", the men refused to disclose anything other than their name, rank and serial number. Bob recalls having little to eat and spending several days in solitary confinement.

The men boarded 40 x 8 boxcars, intended for 40 men or 8 horses, for the train ride north to Barth, Germany. The ride was not without drama since Allied planes would strafe any train in occupied territory. Eventually they made it to their new home, Stalag Luft I, only 90 miles from Sweden.

Accommodations in the south compound of this prison camp were poor. Men slept on straw mattresses with only a single blanket for warmth. Each room housed 16 men. Heat was provided by a single small stove fueled by their daily ration of a few pieces of coal. Luckily they still had their flying suits but their flight jackets had been taken away. Bob would reside here for the next 16 months.

Their barracks was quite close to the fence so some of the men planned to escape by digging a tunnel. The excavated soil was carried outside each day by the prisoners in their pockets and emptied. Bob laughs when he said, "When the guys finally crawled out, they were met by waiting German guards."

At first food consisted of a ration of bread and sometimes potatoes supplemented by what was included in Red Cross parcels. Powdered milk, dates, chocolate bars, and other items made their prison stay tolerable.

After approximately six months, the men stopped receiving the Red Cross parcels and begun to suffer more as a result of the poor nutrition. It turned out that the guards were now keeping this food. Over the next few months Bob's weight dropped from nearly 190 pounds down to 120 pounds.

There was a radio that circulated through the compound in spite of the efforts of the guards to locate and confiscate it. The BBC broadcast news regularly regarding the course of the war. News of the D-Day invasion had spread even before their guards knew of the historic event.

As Bob recalls, one item in Red Cross parcels that was coveted by the guards were the quality cigarettes. The prisoners would trade these with the guards for needed items. On one occasion, the men obtained some prunes that were mixed with sugar to make a sort of homebrew. It really worked Bob recalls. "We got loaded a couple of times."

In spite of the harsh treatment he believes that they were treated better than POWs in the Pacific theater and he was correct. The man held captive by the Japanese that I interviewed described inhumane treatment and brutality. The Japanese troops considered surrender a disgrace and their treatment of the Allied prisoners reflected this attitude.

In May of 1945, the camp was finally liberated by the Russians after the guards had fled to avoid certain execution. The Germans had brutalized Russian civilians early in the war and the Russians were seeking revenge.

Some cattle were brought to the prisoners to butcher but after the meat was consumed, a lot of them became ill. They could not tolerate this quality of food after months of deprivation.

The prisoners were finally transported from Barth in a massive airlift using American B-17s and flown to camp "Lucky Strike" in Le Havre, France, on May 8, 1945. After one month regaining his strength, Bob was finally shipped back to the United States. Some of the weight he had lost had been regained and this prompted his father-in-law into jokingly asking, "Bob, are you sure you've been in prison camp?"

Many veterans took advantage of the G.I. Bill once they returned home. Bob attended Syracuse University that fall. He eventually obtained a degree in accounting and business administration. Bob nearly completed his CPA requirements before returning to Syracuse University for work on a master's degree in education.

During a successful career in education for the Rochester City School District, Bob and his wife Charlotte raised a son and a daughter.

Now nearly 95 years of age, Bob is still able to get out, socialize and occasionally play a round of golf. He recently told me that he played a lot of poker while in prison camp for scraps of paper IOUs. By the time of liberation, his winnings had reached nearly $5000. All the men agreed to pay up when they returned to the United States. Bob was sure he would never see a dollar of his winnings that is until one day a letter arrived addressed to him. Inside was a check for $200 and a note saying, "I promised to pay up, and here it is."

But they all "paid up" in a way by paying the price for the freedom we enjoy today. Unfortunately too many Americans take this freedom for granted.

On several occasions since retirement, I have met with a number of my former patients for lunch. I find it amusing that most of them will have an alcoholic beverage at this time of day. Some of the drinks are ordered with very specific instructions regarding preparation. Once I commented on this and one of the ex-POWs shared the following story with me.

A group of ex-POWs had just finished participating in a Memorial Day parade and decided that a drink was in order so the group proceeded to a nearby bar. These men usually wore burgundy blazers for these occasions and today was no different. They sat at the bar and placed their orders and the lady bartender served the beverages. Once finished, one of the veterans asked, "How much do we owe you?" She replied and one of the veterans produced a bill to cover the tab on the bar.

The lady took the money and paused, saying, "Why are you all wearing those burgundy jackets?"

One of the gentlemen replied, "We are all former prisoners of war and just participated in a parade."

With that she placed her hand on the bill and slid it back to the veteran saying proudly, "Today, the drinks are on me, gentlemen!"

I had a call recently informing me that Bob's wife of more than seventy years, Charlotte, had passed away. Naturally I attended the calling hours a few days later and understandably Bob looked lost. He had lost both of his children, a son from an automobile accident and a daughter from an illness more recently. Now he had his grandchildren but was otherwise alone. I recalled that he had once told me that after his family, he really loved golf. I thought of this and slowly made my way over to him and extended my condolences. Then I placed my hand on his shoulder and said, "Bob, I thought you should know that I have finally joined a golf league."

I won't forget the smile that slowly appeared on his face as he said, "Doc, I really loved to play golf. I hope you enjoy the game as much as I have."

A smiling Bob in his dress uniform.

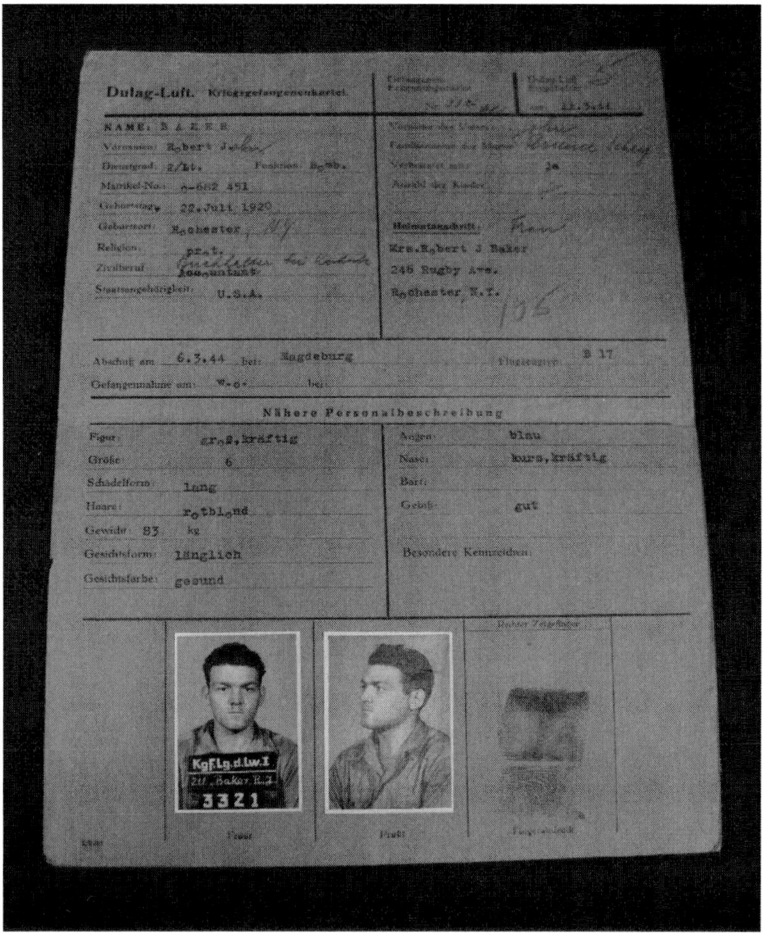

Dulag-Luft. Kriegsgefangenenkartei

NAME: BAKER
Vorname: Robert John
Dienstgrad: 2/Lt.
Matrikel-No.: o-682 451
Geburtstag: 22.Juli 1920
Geburtsort: Rochester, N.Y.
Religion: prot.
Zivilberuf: Accountant
Staatsangehörigkeit: U.S.A.

Verheiratet mit: ja

Heimatanschrift:
Mrs.Robert J Baker
246 Rugby Ave.
Rochester, N.Y.

Abschuß am: 6.3.44 bei: Magdeburg Flugzeugtyp: B 17
Gefangennahme am: w.o. bei:

Nähere Personalbeschreibung

Figur: groß, kräftig
Größe: 6
Schädelform: lang
Haare: rotblond
Gewicht: 83 kg
Gesichtsform: länglich
Gesichtsfarbe: gesund

Augen: blau
Nase: kurz, kräftig
Bart:
Gebiß: gut
Besondere Kennzeichen:

Kgf.Lg.d.Lw.I
2/Lt. Baker R.J.
3321

German Prisoner of War document with Bob's photo.

Bob with his wife Charlotte.

A MOTORCYCLE – GERALD VAN BUREN

Jake was being a bit of a "smartass" when he asked his buddy, the first Sergeant, if he could see a picture of his lovely wife. Jake said, "Boy, is she beautiful! Can I have one of your candy bars?"

A direct hit two days later killed that first Sergeant and a Captain, both his good friends. After that, he vowed never to get close with any other men in his unit. Losing friends was just too painful.

Gerald "Jake" Van Buren was born in November 25, 1917, in Penn Yan, New York, and joined the Army on March 12, 1941, nine months before Pearl Harbor. One can only guess as to why young men joined before the war began but possibly the events occurring in Europe influenced their decision to do so. After he completed Basic Training at Fort Belvoir, Virginia, Jake was sent on to Fort Bragg, North Carolina, for more training. He was considered to be very smart, having a high IQ, and he was asked to do clerical work in the office. Now he was able to assign other young men various jobs such as guard duty and KP the kitchen police. Jake usually picked what he called the "foul balls" or troublemakers for the unpleasant kitchen duties.

Months went by and his work continued to be easy, that is until the United States was finally drawn into the war. The men in his unit boarded a ship, bound for North Africa where the British and German forces were locked in vicious combat. After two weeks crossing the Atlantic Ocean, they finally anchored nearly 4 miles from shore near Casablanca. Along with several other men in a reconnaissance team, Jake moved slowly toward shore in a very small boat. They had their weapons and one American flag that Jake carried. Once they had safely landed, Jake climbed a tree and attached "Old Glory". It was November 8, 1942, and these were the first Americans to land in North Africa and join the war. Over the next few hours, more men from the ship continued to land until there was a huge explosion. His ship with all of his belongings had been torpedoed but luckily most of the men aboard were rescued.

During the next month there was considerable contact with the enemy. On one occasion, he came upon a German and both young men carefully aimed at each other but did not immediately fire. Jake hollered, "Go home" and the German, obviously more terrified, turned and ran away.

His other responsibility, along with the captain, was to censor all outgoing mail from the troops so that vital information about their location and mission was not disclosed. Some were really quite amusing.

Jake was able to drive all of the Army vehicles by this time and when their motorcycle reconnaissance man was injured, Jake was asked to fill in. This turned out, unfortunately, to be more than a temporary assignment.

His unit, Company B, 36th Engineer Regiment, moved on to Sicily where Jake was temporarily assigned to drive a 2 1/2 ton truck. His job was to carry supplies for the rapidly advancing infantry. The Allied forces gained control of the island in only 28 days before turning their attention northward to the beachheads of Anzio, Italy. Of all his experiences during the war, this would be remembered as "pure hell - terrible."

There was so much resistance from the enemy that all the troops were terrified. Jake remembers some of the soldiers deliberately injuring themselves in order to be sent back home. The Germans were hitting them with everything including the dreaded 88s that exploded with deadly accuracy. Most of the men in his unit eventually were either shot or hit by exploding shrapnel. Their cook was so afraid, that he could not leave his tent during a strafing attack until Jake dragged him into his foxhole. "You saved my life," the cook said when the tent was hit several times. After the war he would name his firstborn, a girl, after Jake, Gera Lyn.

Jake recalls several instances when men nearby were killed. There was one soldier who showed off a picture of his new baby and said, "I am going to live to see this baby." Two days later he was killed. Another man simply snuck out of his foxhole with toilet paper to go to the bathroom before meeting the same fate. Jake said he remembers losing his good friends, the first Sargent and Captain, with whom he worked so closely. After both men were killed by a direct hit on their tent, the command post, he would never be the same. From that point on he vowed never to get close to another man. After at least 60 days of combat, the battle finally ended and the Allied troops moved further into Italy.

His unit was eventually sent on to France to join the other Allied troops after the D-Day invasion. Jake or "Van" as he was known to some of the officers, was once more on his motorcycle delivering messages and doing reconnaissance. Again there was considerable contact with the enemy. In spite of the fact that the Germans were losing ground quickly, Jake continued to be shot at frequently.

Once, while out doing reconnaissance on his motorcycle, he nearly ran into some Germans and only escaped by rolling the bike into a ditch. They obviously thought they had shot him but this was not the case. Trying to lift the heavy motorcycle after they left seemed almost impossible but he succeeded and made it back without further incident.

Jake remembers a few events that in combat were unusual. On the first occasion, he captured a German soldier while out on reconnaissance. After binding the hands of the enemy, he had him climb aboard his motorcycle for a ride back to Battalion and interrogation. The other occurred when he heard some rounds hit very close to him on two consecutive days while he was riding by a house. Jake suspected that the shots were coming from Germans hiding in that house and requested that some mortar rounds be fired in that direction. As soon as the mortars hit, the enemy soldiers promptly surrendered. Jake asked them if they were trying to hit him as he drove by. The captured soldiers laughed and said, "If we wanted to hit you, we would have." They only wanted to surrender.

As he began moving into Germany, Jake's luck finally ran out. While out on a reconnaissance run on his motorcycle, Jake and three soldiers trailing in a Jeep were suddenly ambushed by the Germans. One of the men in the Jeep was hit in the leg but Jake was hit three times, twice in the shoulder and once in the back of the head. He was down but at least he was alive. The Germans promptly took him prisoner and put him in a cellar filled with coal. Jake leaned his head against the "cool" coal in an attempt to stop the bleeding and lessen the pain. After two days, he was taken to the house of a German doctor who dressed his wounds.

Jake recalls the doctor saying in perfect English, "I will do what I can for you." He also said that his wife's brother-in-law was in the United States Army. Jake could feel the bone fragments crackling in the back of his head while the wound was being cleaned and dressed by the doctor. The German said that he could not however stop the pain nor prevent infection but, as it turned out, he had done enough to save Jake's life.

Over the next several weeks the prisoners marched along with their captors as they retreated further into Germany. His estimate is that they walked between 8 to 10 miles each day. Each man received two slices of German brown bread daily along with water. This was just enough to sustain them. Eventually they reached Heidelberg where Jake and some of the other prisoners stayed in the hospital. The men who had not been wounded worked cleaning rooms and operating facilities there. Since Jake had his arm in a sling he was not expected to help. Some of the German officers were rough on the prisoners while some were decent to them. One in particular, named Hans, approached Jake near the end and as they shook hands said, "For you the war is over but I must do my duty and return to the front lines."

The Allied forces were rapidly advancing by this time and one day the men were directed to again move on but this time Jake refused. "Nix me!" One German officer drew his pistol and ordered him to move on. Jake turned to the other prisoners and said that he didn't believe the German would shoot them and he was correct. The officer finally turned away and left the remaining prisoners behind.

After a few days, Jake and the other prisoners began to hear the distinctive sound of approaching armor. They rushed to the windows and beheld the beautiful sight of an American tank and halftrack approaching. They were free at last!

Gerald Van Buren returned to Penn Yan after the war, married and raised a family. He had a long and successful career selling automobiles. For many years, I provided care to Jake as his dentist at the nearby Veteran's Hospital. He was always gracious and very appreciative of what we did for him and that always seemed ironic to me, considering all he had done for his country. He's gone now but I still have that special picture of him astride his motorcycle, smiling as usual, and the same picture that proudly hangs on the wall of the American Legion.

I remember one of Mr. Van Buren's visits in particular where we spoke about the dental treatment he had received over the years as a former prisoner of war. The VA actually has very specific eligibility requirements that entitle veterans for health care. Since he had been a prisoner during wartime he did qualify. I asked him about other benefits he received. His reply that the dental care and periodic medical checkups were the only benefits he was receiving which really surprised me. He was not receiving any compensation beyond this. "Do you mean that you are not getting any disability compensation from the government even after being shot three times and loosing part of your skull?" I asked not even mentioning the PTSD issues that most combat veterans deal with.

"No," was Jake's reply.

"I think you should pursue this. If anyone deserves disability benefits, you do," I firmly stated.

Several weeks later a now very pleased veteran proclaimed, "Doc, I need to thank you. Because of you, I will now be getting 100% disability from the VA."

"Oh no, Mr. Van Buren. Please don't thank me. What you will now be finally receiving you earned 65 years ago."

Young Jake in uniform

Jake seated on his motorcycle

Gerald "Jake" Van Buren, a few years ago and still smiling.

SMELLS, SOUNDS – LIONEL METIVIER

"Who the hell are you?" shouted General Patton as "Frenchie" snapped to attention and saluted. Lionel Metivier was dressed proudly in a ski outfit his mother had recently sent from home in northern New Hampshire. When you grow up in that part of New England, you learned very early to ski and probably also to speak French fluently.

I first encountered this interesting veteran, who now goes by the name "Hap", while helping a dentist friend in his private practice. He said, "You're going to love this guy."

I entered the waiting room to greet this gentlemen who was sitting with another veteran who was already my patient at the Veterans Hospital. Don, a Vietnam veteran was surprised. "What are you doing here? "He asked.

"Oh, I am just helping out," and proceeded to introduce myself to "Hap".

And so began my relationship with Lionel. He became my patient and my friend.

"Hap" was born in New Hampshire where he claims his "crib language" was French. He grew up learning "things like skiing and winter survival techniques."

Lionel was drafted into the United States Army shortly after graduating from high school in 1944. His class would be the last to go to war in Europe. After completing basic training at Camp Blanding, Florida, he was sent to Boston to begin the long journey across the Atlantic. The huge French liner, "SS Ile de France", was considered to be much faster than enemy subs and escorting ships were unnecessary. Lionel got along with the French crew and therefore was able to obtain special treatment for him and his buddies. They began calling him "Frenchie" and the nickname stuck throughout his combat tour in Europe.

He crossed the English Channel in an LSD in January 3, 1945. This vessel was a troop transport approximately 200 feet long. The ride made many of the men seasick but was considerably easier than it had been for the troops who landed the previous June for the D-Day invasion. His unit landed in Le Havre and the some of the men asked if he could help them find some drinking water. Lionel approached an elderly French lady and proceeded to ask her where they could get some fresh water. She was very surprised and said, "Oh my little boy- you speak the old French of my grandparents!" His ability to speak French would prove very helpful to the men in the days ahead.

The weather had been unseasonably warm for January, but this soon changed as they began their journey to Alsace Lorraine traveling in a 40 x 8 boxcars. These were intended to carry either 40 men or eight horses. Lionel discovered that he was one of the few men who know how to deal with the cold. He had learned in survival training as a youth to wrap newspaper abound his body under the clothing. The other men were shown how to layer the paper under their poplin field jackets and pants for protection from the bitter cold. After three days in transit they arrived at their destination, Alsace Lorraine.

The men would serve as replacements for the men lost three days prior. They were now members of the 79th Division, 314th Regiment, Easy Company. They checked in at headquarters located in an old building and immediately the sergeant screamed, "Hit the deck!" as a mortar attack commenced. Frenchie was introduced to war at that very moment. The date was January 7, 1945. This was near the end of the Battle of the Bulge and, while the Germans were retreating, their company was under constant harassment by the enemy.

"They were fighting as diligently as they could," Frenchie remembers.

Lionel's first exposure to the formidable German 88 mm occurred when his unit was looking for a Panzer that had taken out several Sherman tanks with its armor piercing rounds. The GIs had only bazookas and the worthless 57 mm antitank gun. The deadly -88- was used as an artillery piece, as an antiaircraft gun and on certain German tanks. The sound of the 88, a crack, was terrifying to the Allied forces. "If you heard it, it was too late."

Many of the details of this terrible battle are often not shared by the combat veterans. Frenchie recalls that one young GI was a German Jew who detested the Nazis. One day while they standing in a church yard next to several snow covered German corpses, this GI began to urinate on the face of one of the dead men saying, "I wonder what this S...O...B.... looks like." He was never allowed to escort captured German soldiers to the rear for fear that he would execute them.

Frenchie claims that, "We had already had that experience with him."

As replacements, these young men were, at best, tolerated by the other men in the company who had lost so many of their buddies. Forming close ties to any of the replacements was discouraged except in the case of Frenchie. He proved to be an asset to the company in combat since he was fluent in French and also some German. Essentials such as food, drinking water, and even liquor could be located easily. Knowing where the Germans had been and might now be was a valuable resource to the other GIs. Lionel remembers sleeping on a dung heap attempting to stay warm as he celebrated his 19th birthday while in Alsace Lorraine.

The 79th division, also known as the Lorraine Division, had been in combat since June 19th, 1944, and had suffered significant casualties. The division was finally relieved by the 82nd Airborne Division and sent back to Nance, France. This occurrence was mentioned in the series "Band of Brothers" when they arrived to relieve the 79th boys. Finding the place to stay in Nance was up to the men but Frenchie was able to locate a beautiful château that the Germans had once occupied. Two squads were able to stay in the luxurious residence with a beautiful fireplace. Lionel enjoyed his first bath since entering combat weeks earlier.

His outfit was soon transferred to Trebek, The Netherlands to prepare to cross the Roer River. Two languages were spoken in this region - French and German Dutch. Frenchie was able to locate a French speaking family to stay with for several days prior to crossing the river. Once their training was completed, the troops crossed the river. The Germans were retreating but continued to fight. Mortar attacks were common, but there was little if any strafing by the now weakened Luftwaffe.

On March 21, the British and American forces prepared to cross the Rhine River to Wessel. Frenchie recalls being in his foxhole surrounded by snow and ice. When skiing as a youth he had learned to always carry extra socks with him. The soiled pair could be washed and wrapped around one's body to dry while the second pair went into service. Keeping your feet dry was very important and he taught many of his buddies how to avoid trench foot during these cold damp days. During the war many GIs suffered with this aliment with some resulting in the necessity of amputation of the affected limb.

The 79th Division was now a part of the Patton's Third Army and abutted the British forces to the north. The "Brits" knew about the Americans' C and K rations and were eager to trade for these food sources, especially the coffee. The K rations were like a modern day crackerjack box containing high-protein food. The C ration box was much larger and could feed a man for 30 days or 30 men for one day. It held various items such as cans of stew, eggs and bacon, chocolate bars, cigarettes, and coffee. When the Americans did swap with the British the food they received was often too greasy to eat.

The artillery barrage, the largest bombardment to that point in the war, commenced at about 2 a.m. and lasted nearly three hours. The ground shook continuously during this barrage upon the enemy on the other side. At around 0500 the men boarded the assault boats. In spite of his anxiety at the time, Lionel noticed something shiny near where he was sitting. This was a brass plate that said Gray Marine Company, Penn Yan, New York. After the war, he lived very near this small town in upstate New York but by then the business had closed.

As luck would have it, the crossing was uneventful since the previous wave of men had already secured a nearly thousand yard beachhead.

The Allied forces were moving more quickly now with town after town falling. The retreating enemy now consisted mainly of young boys 15 to 16 years of age but they were dangerous nonetheless. Many were armed with a Panzer Faust, like the American bazooka, to attack the Allied tanks. After a few bad experiences the Allies began throwing their grenades into each cellar they encountered in case the Germans were hiding there. Church steeples were a favorite hiding place for enemy snipers and each time a new one was spotted, it was quickly hit by Allied artillery fire.

Frenchie recalls an older man in his outfit they called "Pop". He was "about 35 years old. Early on, he had told Lionel that, "If you want to go home, follow me and do what I do and don't ask any questions." Pop was like a guardian angel. He had a sixth sense regarding danger. One day he heard a plane approaching and said, "It's not one of ours, take cover." They did not get hit by the strafing Me109 and watched as the plane was eventually shot down.

One town the men entered was devastated. It was Easter Sunday and the men noticed a church that appeared untouched. Lionel and a friend entered this church with their rifles slung over their shoulders. After the two soldiers began to do "the Stations of the Cross", the Germans civilians realized these GIs meant them no harm and allowed them to participate in their Easter service. As they moved through the town, they discovered another building standing that was familiar to all of the GIs. It was a Woolworth's Five and Dime. Anyone that is a member of the baby boomer generation remembers that these were as common here in the United States as the Walmart is today.

Along the way, Lionel had acquired a new friend - a golden retriever who they named Fritz. The dog only understood German but sided with the GIs from this point on.

As they neared Essen and Dortmund, they learned that President Roosevelt had died. The Germans civilians could not understand why they were not weeping. The men explained to them that they will have a new president soon. The men were becoming de-sensitized to the concept of death.

They continued their advance until stopped and informed that the war was finally over. They began celebrating by throwing their grenades into a swimming pool nearby. One man shouted, "It's about the time the bastards gave up."

Soon the men discovered some slave labor camps containing mainly Polish and Russian women. They had been working in German factories. These people were starving and needed to be cared for. Frenchie met a German girl at a dance there who had worked at one of the factories operated by her father who was a Nazi. The father had been killed by the soldiers but the daughter was spared for she had been kind to the Russian and Polish women working for him.

Dances were held for the jubilant GIs and these women were invited. Frenchie recalls the GIs teaching the women how to jitterbug and the women teaching the men how to polka. Refreshments were limited to Coke and some sweets but they all had a good time.

During World War II, the Americans would earn points for their time in combat and since Frenchie had not yet acquired enough points to go home he was reassigned. He joined the First Infantry Division in the Sudetenland in Czechoslovakia. A student of the war will recall that the 1st Division landed along with the 29th on D-Day in France. Their job there was to identify people of German ancestry who had been living there and return them to Germany. Some of the families had lived in the region for over 100 years. On one occasion, Frenchie and two other GIs went to a bar for a drink where they met some civilians who said they were communists. These men told the Americans that the Americans would soon be kicked out of Czechoslovakia and that the Russians would take over. The predictions were realized with time.

Lionel eventually received orders to travel to Munich for an unusual assignment which was to be his last. The town of Garmisch-Partenkirchen in Bavaria had wonderful ski slopes. Since the occupation forces needed some recreation, the decision was made to teach them how to ski. He informed his superiors that he already knew how to ski. Lionel was selected to attend a ski school so he could serve as an instructor. He was provided a ski shop and a couple of men to assist him. One was German and one was Hungarian. Lionel contacted his mother back in New Hampshire and asked her to send some of his ski clothing for this new assignment. Each Sunday evening nearly 250 GIs arrived and departed the following Saturday after enjoying themselves on the slopes. Lionel remembers racing with his German friend Karl down the Zugspitze once the class had reached the summit.

Things were going well for him now that he was doing something he really loved. He proudly wore his ski sweater decorated with deer and snowflakes. It unfortunately clashed with the black belt he had acquired adorned with a swastika buckle. Word spread quickly one day that General Patton was coming to town for an inspection of all the men on duty from the Third Army. With sirens blaring and flags waving the General and his entourage arrived. The door to the shop flew open and General Patton strutted in followed by his adjutants. Lionel, dressed in his ski outfit, came to attention and saluted the general. General Patton looked him in the eye and shouted, "Who the hell are you?"

"Corporal Metivier, Sir," was the reply.

"What the hell are you? You are out of uniform." Patton continued.

"I'm the ski instructor, Sir." was his sheepish response.

Patton turned to some of his adjutants and said, "Get this guy ski wear that looks official!" With that he wheeled around and left.

The new uniform with military insignia arrived and Lionel wore it proudly while working as a ski instructor until he was discharged from active duty a year later. He continued to reside in Germany, however, for another year. He enjoyed sailing in the summer and skiing in the winter, that is, until he broke his leg severely. It was finally time to return home to the United States.

Lionel completed college in New Hampshire and went on to receive a Masters and PhD at the University of Michigan. His dream of becoming a college professor was realized and he enjoyed a long and successful career in education.

He had somehow survived the war in which his 79th Division had suffered tremendous losses. Over 10,000 men were wounded and 2,475 were killed in action. Lionel vividly remembers the feeling of adrenaline pumping through his body in combat, always feeling ready, ready to react to any sharp sound, even to this day. He also cannot forget the devastation he witnessed in France, Belgium, and Germany during the war. He had experienced "the best and worst mankind is capable of."

Lionel "Frenchie" Metivier is very proud of his service to his country as a member of a division of very gallant men whose insignia was the gray Lorraine Cross on a blue shield, the "Cross of Lorraine".

Nearly seventy years have passed since Hap participated in World War II and, as might be expected, he seldom thinks about what transpired.

That is unless prompted by certain odors, what he refers to as the "smell of war". The smell of cordite from exploding gunpowder filled the air during intense combat as did the odor emanating from the dead bodies scattered about. And lastly the smell of human perspiration, not so much from physical exertion, but from fear surrounded him. That gripping fear that you may die at any moment.

For all combat veterans, these odors are very significant and quickly result in a profound reaction to experiences so long ago.

Hap (right) with a friend after joining the Army.

Left: Hap smiling with his friend 'Fritz' who only understood German Below: Hap wearing the uniform from General Patton.

Taking a break with two other ski instructors

THE WEDGE – CHARLES COREA

A flash came from the waist gunner of the bomber nearby.
Fighters were attacking from directly above the formation. The three closest B-17s were ablaze after the first pass. As another Me109 banked, he was no more than 20 feet from Charlie's plane. The twin 50's could not miss. The eyes of the fighter pilot and this top turret gunner met for just an instant as debris from the fighter's tail section blew away. The Hundredth Bomb Group or "Bloody Hundred" was about to pay a terrible price for this mission to Berlin, Germany.

I first met Charlie, also known to his buddies as "The Wedge", approximately twenty years ago when the government decided that former prisoners of war should have their dental care provided by the Veterans Administration. I will never forget that first appointment when I began examining the high quality dental care that he had received and he stated firmly. "All of this work was done by my golf buddy, Straz. So if you screw anything up, I always have him to bail you out." Then he began to laugh. He somehow found some humor in most everything he experienced in life.

Charlie Corea graduated from East Rochester High School the year before the Pearl Harbor attack. The United States soon finds itself at war. After playing cards all night, Charlie and some friends arrived at the draft board office at promptly 6 a.m. and signed up for the service. Charlie was first in line. It was September of 1942, and soon Charlie would find himself at Fort Niagara for both physical and written examinations. One portion of the eye test did not go well. He was found to be colorblind. Before arrangements could be made for another test, however, he was sent to Atlantic City for basic training.

Air Corps aptitude examinations were given and Charlie qualified for all possible assignments. Aerial photography seemed like a good choice for this young airman. Instead, he was given his second choice, and began aircraft mechanics training after arriving in Goldsboro, North Carolina. He had convinced his friend, who wanted to become a radioman, to select aerial photography as a second choice. As luck would have it, his friend was trained as a photographer. After the war, that friend continued with this profession and was very successful.

While in Goldsboro, North Carolina, Charlie again took and passed the color vision test for aerial gunnery. After the war, a friend reminded Charlie that he had taken the test for Charlie, but strange things happened during war time that were not always remembered.

While the war was raging in Europe and the Pacific, Charlie felt like he was on vacation. The Great Depression had ended and for the first time in years, there was adequate food for everyone. He was with his friends and away from home. Everywhere the men went they were treated royally by the civilians. The country was united in its support of the war effort. Charlie recalls that when hitchhiking, "The first car always stopped for servicemen." He remembers that in those days, "everyone wanted to do something for the country."

The men and women of his generation had grown up during the '30s when times were tough for everyone. Most of their fathers were not working consistently and any money the children earned was shared with the family. They all managed to just get by with limited food and hand-me-down clothing. Beds were usually shared with siblings for most of the children were members of large families. Early on, Charlie worked as a caddy at a local golf course and earned 65 cents for working eighteen holes. Later on his salary increased to $20 per week for stoking a furnace in a nearby factory. Of this sum, $15 was given to his mother to help support their family.

My father shared similar stories with me about the depression. When he went into the service, it was the first time he could remember having enough to eat and adequate clothing. In many ways, having endured the Great Depression had prepared this generation for the hardship and sacrifices the war would bring.

Gunnery school at Fort Myers, Florida, was the next stop for Charlie where he enjoyed skeet shooting the most. The men would ride in the rear of pickup trucks and attempt to hit clay pigeons launched at random along the side of the road. Also, he could assemble and disassemble a 50 caliber machine gun blindfolded after the five weeks of training. Before leaving for his next assignment, he was promoted to corporal.

Curtis Wright Field in St. Louis was the location for the construction of the SP2C1 or dive bomber. This plane had a two man crew, a pilot and engineer/gunner. Charlie studied hydraulics as part of his training and received his second promotion. He was now Sergeant Corea.

In the meantime, the Allies were suffering terrible losses in Europe so the war needs changed. Charlie was shipped to Lake Moses, Washington, to become a crew member of a B-17 or "Flying Fortress". On this new plane, an electrical system replaced the hydraulic system he had recently studied and he was now designated as the first engineer. Charlie enjoyed the training flights over the Columbia River nearly as much as liberty when they partied nearby.

The men were able to travel to Yakima, Washington, with three day passes Charlie forged. The only servicemen returning from combat at that time were from the Philippines. A buddy used to show off his appendix scar to impress the young ladies claiming it was a war wound.

Being a member of a crew with nine other airmen meant operating as a team. Working together was nothing new for Charlie for as a teenager he delivered milk with his father. The milk wagon was drawn by an old horse up and down the streets of East Rochester. While his father was making deliveries on one side of the road. Charlie would do the same on the other. After completing one street they would move to the next portion of their route sometimes cutting through yards. Their horse would always be waiting for them with the wagon in tow at the appropriate location.

The crew trained for considerable time together and Charlie remembers a few funny stories from those early flights. On one of the "navigation" flights, an inexperienced radioman was assigned to go with them as a sub. Only Charlie, the pilot, copilot and navigator were really necessary so the other men had the night off. Once they had reached the designated altitude, the autopilot was engaged. There was really nothing for the men to do but listen to Glen Miller and take a nap. The copilot laid down near the rookie radioman and fell asleep. This prompted him to call the pilot above but there was no reply. When he went to investigate, he discovered that the pilot was also asleep. He panicked and ran to Charlie screaming, "Everybody's sleeping!"

Charlie began laughing and calmly replied, "Everything's ok. Go back to your radio."

The B-17G, was defended with eleven 50 caliber machine guns operated by several men on the plane: a bombardier, two waist gunners, a top turret man, the tail gunner and a ball turret gunner below. This last position was usually a man of smaller stature who, it was later discovered, could become trapped within the ball if the hydraulic controls were damaged in combat. There was a radio operator who also had access to a gun but rarely used the weapon. The navigator, pilot and copilot completed the ten man crew. All of the men had assigned responsibilities and the success of the mission required cooperation. When flying in tight formations, the planes' defenses were considered formidable. They proved to be vulnerable, however, to antiaircraft fire and the much faster enemy fighter planes when on bombing missions over Europe.

In January of 1944, Charlie and his crew left for Europe via the northern route. After stops in Newfoundland, Greenland, Iceland, and Scotland, they reached their destination, Thorpe Abbots, England. Because of losses being suffered by the Eighth Air Force at that time, many of the arriving crews were broken up to serve as replacements for existing crews. Charlie's crew joined the 349th Squadron and, along with three other squadrons of 12 planes each, would comprise the 100th Bomb Group. As time passed this group suffered tremendous casualties and was nicknamed "The Bloody Hundred". For a few weeks this group was not able to fly missions since so many of the planes had been lost in combat.

Some of the veterans I have known have stated that the 100th Bomb Group was specifically targeted by the Luftwaffe because of an incident early in the war. One bomber, according to a former pilot, was hit, left formation and appeared to surrender. As enemy fighter planes prepared to escort the wounded B-17 down, the gunners on the bomber suddenly opened fire on the enemy planes. The bomber was then able to escape but breaking this "rule of engagement" would lead to the heavy losses later. I actually witnessed a near altercation between two elderly veterans, both named Charlie, one day when one called the other a "G...D...Fool" for what The Bloody Hundredth had done. My Charlie was not even yet a member of the bomb group when the incident supposedly occurred.

Plans were soon made for the first daylight bombing raid to Berlin, Germany. After a failed attempt that was interrupted by bad weather, they were ready to go on March 6, 1944. With 810 bombers participating, this would be considered a maximum effort. Since Charlie's plane was being repaired, some of his crew would serve as replacements and borrow a plane from the 351st Squadron for the mission. They had lost an engine on the previous mission and had to abort. Whenever this happened, the bombs, machine guns and ammunition were discarded to lessen their weight so they could return safely to base.

While he was responsible for the top turret as crew chief, he was also required to log everything that occurred on each mission and deal with mechanical problems when they arose. Charlie therefore spent much of his time up front with the pilot, copilot, bombardier and navigator. He was closer naturally to these men than the rest of the crew but loyal nonetheless to everyone on board.

The mission, Charlie's fifth, began uneventfully with his plane circling after takeoff until all the planes were airborne. Usually the adventuresome nature of the young men would overtake the potential for what could happen on a mission. At this age, they felt invincible. After briefing on this particular day, however, and discovering what the mission would be, Charlie suddenly lost his appetite. Soon they are on their way to Berlin, Germany, the heart of the Third Reich. This would not be a "milk run" or mission with little danger.

Because they had borrowed this particular plane, they were unfortunately going to have to fly at the end of the formation of planes known as "tail end Charlie", a very vulnerable location. Attacking Me109s and FW180s always attacked the edges of the formation. With all of the United States missions being daytime missions, the attacking bombers were easily seen by the enemy defenders. While Allied fighter planes would escort the "heavy bombers" for the early part of the mission, this protection would not continue far into Germany because of their limited fuel supply.

As they neared their target, the attack from above commenced. Nearly 40 enemy fighters swooped down from directly above onto their group. The midday sun would prevent detection of these enemy planes until it was nearly too late. The first two squadrons were ready for them so the fighters wisely struck the bombers at the rear. The three B-17s in front of Charlie's plane were hit immediately. He was facing the plane's rear in his turret since this was the most vulnerable area for the last bomber in the formation. Seeing the flash from a waist gunner above, he immediately turned in that direction. As one of the Me109s banked to attack again he passed within 20 feet to the right of Charlie in the top turret. The fighter was so close the young airman could not miss. He had him "dead to nuts". For an instant he looked "eye to eye" with that pilot. He began firing and hitting the tail section of the German's plane but then the unthinkable happened. The electrical cord in his flight suit became tangled in the turret mechanism and jammed it. He could not follow the target any farther with his twin machine guns. As he moved down to untangle the cord, Charlie noticed a fire in their plane that he quickly extinguished. He returned to his turret a few moments later only to find it was no longer there. The enemy plane had returned and blown the turret completely off the top of his B-17.

While trying to determine his next move, the bombardier named Tom said, "Charlie, what the f… are we going to do?" Charlie's response was, "What do you want from me? Bail out."

With that, Tom kicked out the front hatch and bailed out, a move that would ultimately save Charlie's life. In the nose of the B-17 where the navigator and bombardier were flying, there is an escape hatch behind the #2 prop to be used in the case of an emergency. If this could not easily be opened, trapped crew members could die. Somehow, the hatch opened and out he went. Unfortunately Tom's loose flying boots blew off when he pulled his rip cord. With the outside temperature at minus 51 degrees, he suffered severely frozen feet by the time he landed.

For about 5 minutes, nothing happened until the fighters resumed their attack. Charlie had just said to the pilot, "Kop, dive into the clouds." The number three engine was hit next and burst into flames. On their next pass the fighters shot out the controls sending the bomber into a downward spiral upside down. Bailing out under these conditions would be nearly impossible because of the G forces the men were subjected to.

Charlie grabbed the chest pack parachute but was unable to get it on due to the spiraling of the plane. He finally was able to attach it in front of his "Mae West" life vest. He could see the ground coming fast and then suddenly fell out of the open hatch head first. He could never have kicked out the hatch under the circumstances. Thank God Tom had already done so. While exiting the plane, the prop of the number two engine smashed his left foot and split it open. Luckily, the copilot followed him out but the rest of the crew were not as fortunate. The bomber loaded with tons of explosives crashed only about 400 yards away. The bombardier had helped the injured navigator, Lieutenant Wing, put his chest pack on but he "froze" and was unable to escape. Years after the war, the navigator's mother paid Charlie a visit trying to learn how her son had died. Seven of the ten man crew had perished on this mission.

Of the 34 planes flying from the 100th Bomb Group on this mission, most never reached and bombed the target. Mechanical problems had forced four to return to their base. These four were very fortunate because half of the remaining B-17s attacking Berlin were shot down by the enemy during the approach. The surviving 15 planes were forced to join the other bomb groups for safety and only one actually landed at the base from which it had departed that morning. In all, 69 heavy bombers and 11 fighters were lost on that first mission to bomb Berlin, Germany.

Charlie and the copilot, Gordon Lien, hit the ground near a farmhouse where people had been hiding during the terrifying attack. With this many bombers in the air, the attack could last for up to three hours. The copilot asked one of the farmers where they were. His response was "Deutschland". Even though Gordon was of German ancestry, he responded, "We are in luck, we're in Holland." Charlie shouted, "Deutschland's not Holland!" The response had seemed funny to Charlie at the time until he noticed blood spurting from his right foot. A farmer arriving on the scene went into Charlie's harness and found a tourniquet which he applied to the injured leg. Some sulfa powder, also there, was applied to the wound. It was hard to believe that a German was now providing first aid to the enemy who was bombing his country. Soon the bombs that were still on his plane began to explode nearby and the people ran for cover. The civilian guard arrived as this was happening and Charlie and Gordon were taken prisoner.

After being taken to an infirmary in a small community nearby, Charlie's two nearly severed toes were amputated and the foot was bandaged. He was then taken to a hospital. This was a Luftwaffe hospital caring for injured German airmen but they operated on Charlie nonetheless. He recalled the two doctors saying that, "We are doctors first and soldiers second."

Charlie remained in that hospital for nearly a month and a half. This facility would periodically come under aerial attack. When the air raid siren commenced, all of the recovering German airmen were moved to a more protected location but the enemy patients were left behind. Since Charlie was now able to hop about a little, he would search through the German's belongings and steal a cigarette or two for his friends to enjoy. Each time before the Germans returned, Charlie would return to his bed.

On Easter Sunday 1944, the hospital was again attacked but this time the "targets of opportunity" for Allied P-47 thunderbolts were two JU88s, medium bombers, hidden under trees nearby. Charlie could see the fighters attacking from east to west and described the action for the other American prisoners. He found it amusing when the very loud 50 caliber machine guns on the planes were answered by one puny 30 mm gun in the tower nearby. All went well until the P-47s changed their direction and began strafing from north to south hitting the hospital operating room but narrowly missing their ward. This would be the second attack from the air he was to survive but this time it was by Allied planes.

One day during his transfer to Frankfurt, Germany, he and some other prisoners were sitting down along the road when a very attractive German girl approached on a bicycle. She stopped and said, "Well the war is over for you guys at least." The civilians were obviously suffering a great deal from the continuous Allied bombing of their homeland.

Charlie was then interrogated in Frankfurt and eventually sent to Stalag 17b in Austria near the Switzerland border. There were nearly 4200 other enlisted men held as prisoners there. With his leg not yet healed he was placed in an infirmary in the camp and remained there for almost 10 months. He felt that he was treated a little better than the other prisoners in the compounds during this time.

While confined at this prison, the prisoners were given one Red Cross parcel per week. The parcel contained spam, biscuits, a 2 ounce can of coffee, dried milk also known as "klim", a quarter pound of cheese, five packs of cigarettes and two chocolate bars known as "D" bars. This was supplemented by the black bread provided by the guards that contained 20% sawdust. The prisoners regularly traded the cigarettes with Russian prisoners in the compound nearby for vegetables. The Russian prisoners were allowed to work on farms during the day and managed to sneak fresh carrots, potatoes and onions back into their compound. The trading worked as long as the items, which were thrown over the fence, did not land between the main fence and the warning wire 20 feet inside. Anyone entering this "no man's land" could be shot. One Russian prisoner was killed by the guards as he attempted to retrieve a pack of cigarettes in the forbidden zone.

As the advancing Russian army neared their camp, the Germans set up a defensive position on the hill nearby. The prisoners were in the middle of this firefight until the Germans finally withdrew. The men were now finally free. The Americans there were flown to camp "Lucky Strike" in Le Havre, France.

Charlie eventually returned to the United States and to his home in East Rochester where he married Jeanette, the police chief's daughter. They raised four children and are very proud of their many grandchildren and great-grandchildren.

Over the years, we became close friends, often having dinner with our wives and playing a little golf. Charlie always scheduled his appointments late in the morning so we could either go out for lunch or hit a few golf galls on the VA Hospital's golf course nearby.

I will never forget his call early one morning when he frantically said "Jeff, I broke my front tooth."

I said '"Don't worry Charlie, I will take care of it for you."

When he arrived, I concluded that his tooth could not be saved but made arrangements for my lab to fabricate a temporary appliance during the lunch time. After extracting his tooth and packing gauze on the wound, we decided that we would got out and play some golf. As we were walking out, a young female employee who flirted with many of the men at the hospital was walking in. She looked at us and said, '"Where are you going?"

I looked at her and replied, "Charlie and I are going to play a round of golf."

She smiled and said, "Now that's a dentist I would play a round with too!"

Charlie nearly choked on the gauze and began laughing hysterically.

Even near the end as he was losing his battle with cancer, Charlie always felt good enough for my visits.

When his time finally came, I went for the calling hours. Next to his casket stood his prized golf club, "the Wedge."

Charles Corea always felt after the war that we ultimately won not because we were better than they were. We won because we had more resources than the enemy possessed. This sentiment was repeated many times by other World War II veterans I've cared for over the years. On several occasions since the war when he was interviewed, the person suggested that Charlie was a hero. His response was always the same. "I am not a hero - the guys who did not make it are the real heroes."

Charlie shortly after running into his cousin also in the service

Standing with the pilot and radio operator from his crew.

POW photograph.

Charlie and his wife Jeanette after the war.

A more recent picture of Charlie and Jeanette.

LOYALTY —JOSEPH DIPROJETO

Joseph Cisi carried the bleeding limp body of his friend Joe DiProjeto down the mountainside to the aid station. The captain said, "Put that man over there with the others!" assuming he would soon be dead. Joseph slowly removed his 45 pistol and pointed it at the captain saying, "If you don't put him on that Jeep and take him down right now, I'll blow your f....... brains out!" The captain conceded. But would they really be able to save this man's life?

He is known to his friends as Joe D. and is really a very interesting veteran. To me, he initially came across as a tough guy who would not take "crap" from anyone. But there is also the other side to this man I grew to know; that of a loving loyal family man who would cherish and protect his friends and family without hesitation.

Joe DiProjeto was born in Pennsylvania but after his father died, the family moved back to his mother's hometown of Rochester, New York. Young Joe attended elementary school and then both Washington and Edison Tech high schools. He really enjoyed high school where he was able to play varsity basketball for three years. His life changed, however, in 1943, once he was drafted into the Army. With the country at war, all able-bodied men were required to serve.

Joe's military experience began at Camp Upton, New York, and after a while he was sent to Arkansas where he joined an infantry division. Later, some of the men including Joe, were sent out west to Camp Hale, Colorado, where the division was broken up. Here the men needed to adjust quickly to the new altitude but some of them never did. Rock climbing with the full 90 pound pack was challenging for many of the men. They learned to walk on snow shoes and survive in this mountainous terrain. He recalls bivouacking for two weeks at one point under these harsh conditions. Bedding there consisted of pine boughs spread over the soft snow. Joe and the rest of the men, belonging to what was now known as the 10th Mountain Division, were preparing for combat in the mountainous regions of Europe. This included former Senator Bob Dole who, readers will recall, was severely injured during the war.

Joe was a member of the 85th Regiment but, when two men from the 87th Regiment went AWOL, Joe and another young serviceman were sent as replacements. He knew no one in this new regiment and refused to go. Captain Luther said he had to go. "I am giving you a direct order," said the captain.

Joe told the captain what he could do with the plan and also went AWOL. It was not that he wanted out of the Army, he just wanted to stay with the guys he had trained with. The young soldier made his way all the way to Corpus Christi, Texas, the rendezvous point for the four men. Two weeks later, Sargent Grafi, who knew where they had gone, arrived and convinced young Joe and the others to return to the unit.

In the eyes of the military, this was a serious offense and Joe was certain he would be court-martialed. This would be a special court-martial because he not only went AWOL but swore at an officer. Somehow, he and his friend, Joe Cisi, were reassigned to another company and sent to North Carolina. It was New Year's Eve, 1944, when the 85th and 86th Regiments departed on a troopship bound for Naples, Italy. Nearly 5,000 men were packed like sardines on the ship. Once they arrived in Italy, the men were quickly sent to an area known as "Leghorn" in the mountains. Soon they were climbing hills again but now there was a difference. They were being shot at. The foxholes that had been vacated by the Germans were inviting but the men were told not to use them. They had probably been zeroed in ready to be shot at by the enemy.

It was now early January, 1945, and Joe had become part of a mortar team with the responsibility of carrying the heavy rounds for the mortar. He remembers it being pitch black on a particular night with all the men freezing. Although the Americans were higher on the mountain than the enemy, they were taking heavy rifle and machine gun fire along with numerous mortar rounds from the Germans below. Joe remembers laying in a foxhole and praying, certain he would die that night.

At first light Joe could see the bodies, both German and American, lying everywhere on the mountainside. Some were his buddies. Joe was slowly making his way to the outpost when he heard the distinctive whistle of the dreaded German 88. He was about 50 feet from the outpost where the captain, lieutenant, and two sergeants were, but he quickly jumped into a foxhole with this sound. He landed on top of another guy as the round made a direct hit on the outpost killing everyone inside.

The shrapnel had penetrated his helmet and blown part of his skull away. Although he could hear, he could no longer see and was covered with his own blood. His good friend Joseph Cisi ran to assist him but quickly discovered how seriously injured he was. His buddy slowly carried him down the mountainside only pausing when Germans resumed shelling their position. The captain at the aid station took a quick look at Joe and was sure he was "a goner". "Just lay him over there," he said.

When his buddy heard the captain say to put Joe where there were only bodies of dead men, he refused. He unholstered his 45 and placed it up to the captain's face and threatened him saying, "If you don't strap him on that Jeep, I will blow your f...... brains out." Reluctantly the captain loaded Joe on the vehicle and arranged for someone to drive him for medical treatment. His friend had saved his life.

After undergoing surgery at the hospital, Joe soon began to see blurry images. He spent nearly three months in the hospital before being sent home on a ship. While on route, the injured men received news that their commander-in-chief, FDR, had passed away. All the men were devastated.

Another lengthy hospital stay in Atlantic City followed his arrival in the states where a plate was inserted into his skull. Young Joe could again see clearly but unfortunately the cost of war surrounded him. Here were men who had lost limbs, some both arms and legs, and were convalescing. Joe was sickened by the site of these deformed men being carried out onto the boardwalk in baskets for some sunshine. Unfortunately, the horrible term "basket cases" was used to describe these mutilated veterans.

After being discharged from the Army in August, 1945, Joe returned to Rochester, New York, where he and his bride would eventually raise two sons and a daughter. While he was very strict with his children, he nonetheless wanted nothing but the best for them. When his boys decided as teenagers that they wanted to move out and live in an apartment, Joe's response was, "If you go, don't come back."

As for his daughter, she eventually found a special young man and planned to marry him. Joe told me the story about the day he took him into his basement and said to his future son-in-law, "In 17 years I have never laid a hand on my daughter. Do you see that fireplace in the back yard? If you ever hurt her, you'll be under that fireplace."

Many years after the war, he went to New York City to look up Joseph Cisi, the man who had helped him. He gave his friend a beautiful gold watch that had cost $250, a lot of money in those days, and said, "How can I ever repay you for saving my life?"

All his friend could say was, "Joe, you are a lucky man." Lucky yes, but having a loyal friend had certainly helped.

Joe as a young GI and member of the 10th Mountain Division.

Joe a few years ago.

THE RUNNER – EDWARD SEWARD

Ed Seward was always a very fast runner. In high school he won the county championship in the mile. Now he was drifting slowly earthward in a parachute but there was no way he could outrun the bullets flying in his direction. The year was 1944 and this was no game he was playing.

Growing up in East Rochester, New York, Ed loved playing sports. Football and basketball were fun but his favorite activity was running track. In his spare time he caddied at the Monroe Country Club. One of the members suggested that he apply to Purdue University. He was so successful in the county and sectional meets that financial assistance was available when he entered Purdue University that fall. Ed majored in physical education and continued to participate in track and field. During his first year, he lettered in the sport and as a sophomore won the two-mile race competing against the best from Wisconsin and Michigan State. His roommate at Purdue was a lad named Henry Stram who later on in life went by the name "Hank". You may remember that Hank Stram was the coach of the Kansas City Chiefs in the first Super Bowl.

In November of 1942, one of Ed's fraternity brothers encouraged him to take the test for the Army Air Corps cadet program, which he passed. Before returning to the frat house, however, he had been sworn in with the understanding that he would not have to report for duty until early in 1943. Many of the other guys in the physical education program also joined but his roommate Henry did not make the cut because of his knee problems.

Ed was able to return home for a couple of months before having to finally report for service.

Ed eventually reported to Lackland Air Force Base in San Antonio, Texas, for classification. After scoring very high in the navigation test, he went for his basic training and preflight training. By December of 1943, he had graduated from navigation school, where he trained on the small AT-7, and was shipped to Dalhart, Texas, for B-17 training. Ed briefly went to New Mexico for the B-29 program but then returned to Dalhart to complete the original program. The United States was at war and all the young men were eager to serve their country. "We wanted to get overseas, wanted to get into the war. There was no question about it," Ed recalls. In April of 1944, his wish was granted and he received orders to ship out in May.

After being assigned to the 398th Bomb Group of the Eighth Air Force base in England, a few training missions were completed. The first real challenge would be to fly deep into enemy territory and bomb what was known as "the big B", Berlin, Germany. The men received this information during their 5 a.m. briefing. The plane was boarded by 6 a.m. and departed at nearly 7. Fully loaded with fuel, ammunition, bombs and oxygen tanks, the B-17 Flying Fortress was a huge, flying bomb. Ed was excited initially but later on got a bit nervous for it was his responsibility to guide the plane to and from the target. He was not the lead plane for the mission, but if there were any problems, such as that plane leaving formation, he would be responsible for finding the target and then the way home.

When a target was bombed, it was not approached directly as one might expect. For example, their plane actually flew approximately 20 miles north of Berlin and then at least 10 miles past the city. They next made a right turn flew 20 miles south then another right turn and went 10 miles back towards the target. Initially, as they flew past the city, Ed noticed a huge black cloud hovering over Berlin and asked one of the men if there were going to go through that. The answer from the more experienced airmen was, "Yes, it's flak."

They had been attacked by enemy fighters on route but even the German fighters would not risk flying through the antiaircraft's exploding shrapnel. The bomb run went okay but Colonel Killian's plane nearby was hit and soon engulfed in flames. The crewmen could be seen parachuting out, always a good sign, but Ed was sure the men would not survive descending through that cloud of exploding flak.

A few more missions followed including two to bomb Hamburg, Germany. The men were relieved to discover that the mission for the 25th of June would be a milk run to southern France. This term is used to describe a combat mission where very little if any enemy resistance can be expected. After all, this was weeks after the invasion in Normandy and the Germans were on the verge of being driven out of France. The mission was actually longer than some of the prior missions to Germany because they were heading to southeastern France.

Just west of Paris, the milk run suddenly went sour as the formation was attacked by enemy fighters causing some damage to Ed's plane. Their biggest problem now was that they were losing precious fuel. Ed remembers joking with one of the crew members saying, "There are the Pyrenees Mountains. If we have to bail out, try to make it there." That way one could evade the Germans and reach neutral Spain.

His B-17 was at the end of the formation known as "tail end Charlie". Soon, because of the damage, they were lagging further behind. This made them an inviting target for the enemy below. The plane's number 3 engine was hit and began to burn. Now they were in serious trouble.

Usually the German 88 was used for antiaircraft purposes since it was such an accurate artillery piece. Lines of these guns would fire sequentially with the fuses set to detonate at around 25,000 feet, the height of the attacking B-17s. Ed's plane was obviously singled out since it was now flying nearly half a mile behind the other Allied planes and was promptly hit three more times. The plane was soon in flames with one fire very near where the oxygen was stored under the pilot's compartment.

In the nose of the plane Ed, the navigator, and Lieutenant Gneisien, the bombardier, usually flew with only their chest harness since any attached parachute would restrict movement in such a confined space. They would only clip it on in an emergency. Ed said, "We better get the hell out!" even before the pilot John Godwin gave the official order to "bailout". John then kicked out the nose hatch and surprisingly was the first out of the burning plane. The copilot, radioman, and gunners jumped out through the now open bomb bay doors since the payload had already been released. The crew member with the most difficulty was the ball turret gunner who needed intact hydraulics to raise the ball. The backup plan was for a crew member to manually crank up the suspended ball. With so little time this man often did not survive. Luckily, however, he was able to escape this time with the others.

Airmen are trained to wait until they reach about 2000 feet where there is enough oxygen before deploying their parachute but Ed could not wait. He remembers pulling his cord at about 20,000 feet. As he slowly drifted down, Ed remembered to discard his side arm but for some reason also pulled out his wallet. He checked his PX ration card. It would expire the next day, Monday. Today was Sunday and he was wasting one day. People do strange things when in stressful situations. Soon, however, his full attention was directed below as shots rang out. They were shooting at him as evidenced by the numerous holes in his parachute.

Ed hit the ground hard. Once he came to his senses he could see a German soldier approaching followed by a car containing more soldiers. His wallet was quickly taken from him and he was ordered by the captain to march towards the car. Not understanding German, he thought they wanted him to get in. Ed discovered otherwise when he was promptly kicked for doing so. Ed soon found himself in a shed laying on straw. He remembered that he was wearing his rosary around his neck, a common practice for Catholics in those days, and he decided now would be a good time to pray.

A few hours later he was taken to what appeared to be a resort house where he was reunited with the rest of his crew with the exception of Lieutenant Gneisien who had perished. They were visited by two Luftwaffe pilots for some reason and later by a group of 17 or 18-year-old kids. It turned out that they were the ones who had been manning the 88s. They were arguing and wanted to know which of them had shot down the plane. Obviously Ed and his crew had no answer for them.

The men boarded a train bound for Dulag Luft, the interrogation center in Frankfurt. Ed remembers waiting for a truck there with several other airmen when a crowd of civilians surrounded them. These people thought these were the men that had bombed their city the previous night and began assaulting the prisoners. Ed was lucky and was only hit on the back by an elderly man's cane.

Once his interrogation began, it appeared to Ed that the Germans already knew everything. They knew what city he was from, what high school he had attended, and even the name of one of his teachers and track coach, Mr. Grabowski. "How is Mr. Grabowski doing?" The German asked.

The idea obviously was to get the prisoner to think that they had all the information so the prisoner would open up. One can only speculate as to the source of their information. Ed, however, would only state his name, rank and serial number. Years later Ed remembers what occurred next as being his worst wartime experience: being kept in solitary confinement. There was one small trap door through which some food was provided, with water and three slices of bread per day. Occasionally he received some liquid that potatoes had been boiled in, a soup of sorts, but without the potato. Ed refused to divulge any information in spite of the harsh treatment and after several days was sent to Stalag Luft III in Poland.

Prison camp there consisted of five compounds: North, South, East, West and Center. Ed was sent to Center. At one point there was an escape attempt by some of the British prisoners about which a movie, "The Great Escape", was produced years later. Ironically the first person he met here was Colonel Killian, the man he saw bail out on his very first combat mission and he had presumed had died.

Red Cross parcels containing corned beef, spam, margarine, jam, coffee, D bars, and klim (dried milk) supplemented the meager food rations provided by the Germans. One man was selected from each room to be the cook, to prepare the food and divide it evenly among the men. As the cook, Ed could make pudding from the chocolate D bar and klim for the other prisoners to enjoy. The rations such as spam were very carefully divided into twelve even pieces by the cook and then cards were drawn to see who selected first and hopefully took the biggest piece. The cook had the last choice, unfortunately.

By January, the tide of the war had drastically changed and the Russians were advancing rapidly toward their prison camp. The prisoners were forced to leave quickly one cold snowy night taking only what they could carry with them. Ed remembers wearing a pair of shoes with cardboard soles. After walking for many days and occasionally sleeping in barns, the prisoners finally boarded a boxcar and arrived at Stamlager VII in Moosburg, Germany.

There was little food here and this prison camp was very congested. By this time the men were in very poor physical condition. At last the weather finally broke and spring arrived. One day, Ed was making coffee outside when he heard a shot rang out. Were they shooting at him? He thought it was their German guard, "Popeye" but was not certain. In the distance he noticed a church steeple flying the German swastika. A while later he looked again at the steeple and noticed that the flag had been replaced by the Stars & Stripes. Soon, American tanks arrived. Rather than coming through the gate, they simply plowed right through the retaining fences surrounding the prison. The hatch opened and the soldier hollered. "We're here."

Ed screamed, "Jesus, are we glad to see you!"

Their ordeal was finally over!

General Patton arrived soon thereafter but by this time was only wearing one of his famous pearl handled revolvers. The story was that one had been given at a USO show to an actress, Carol Landis, who had admired his weapons. As Patton walked around the camp and saw the men sleeping on the ground, he said, "Deplorable, deplorable!" The German commandant had been strapped to a chair and General Patton asked the now free prisoners, "How did this guy treat you?" Their response was "terrible" and Patton promptly slapped the German officer. In spite of his being a great battlefield commander, Ed remembers General Patton as being a big man who was a little on the crude side.

Newly liberated Americans were sent to Le Havre, France, and what is known as Camp "Lucky Strike". One day while Ed was recuperating there an officer approached his tent and hollered, "Is anyone here from East Rochester?"

It was Tony Scorza with whom he had gone to high school. Tony tried to feed him some good food, but Ed quickly vomited. It was discovered that anyone who was so malnourished was also unable to tolerate regular food and had to adjust gradually to what Americans take for granted.

After returning to the United States, Ed married his high school sweetheart Beryl, and they raised three wonderful children. He chose to remain in the Air Force and in 1950 completed training to become a pilot.

The opportunity to meet interesting people continued when Ed was stationed at MacDill Air Force Base in Florida under the command of Colonel Paul Tibbets. Colonel Tibbets you may remember had piloted the Enola Gay dropping the atomic bomb on Hiroshima, Japan, in 1945. Ed recalls that Tibbets would not allow any drinking on base until 6p.m. He was very sensitive about this since his bombardier on that historic mission became an alcoholic after the war. Ed ultimately retired from the military after serving his country for 25 years.

Ed Seward finally finished the requirements for his bachelor's and master's degrees and pursued a career in education. Where he taught mathematics is however very interesting, a school for court committed delinquents at Industry, New York. Is it possible that his experiences himself as a prisoner helped him understand these troubled youth and be successful teaching them when many others had failed? Ed noted significant improvement in their performance academically and hopefully helped improve their self-esteem.

Ed recalls an incident where he accidentally left a large sum of money on the front seat of his car on a day when he had to drive a number of these boys from a basketball game back to their sleeping quarters. He did not realize that he had left the money there until the last boy had exited the car and Ed was forced to ask the question, why not one of them had picked up the money. Their response was, "We would never think of stealing from you." These boys respected him too much.

Several years ago, I was in the process of completing some bridgework for this veteran who would be leaving for Florida on Friday of that week. The lab said that the appliance would be ready and delivered later that day. Ed's flight was at 9 a.m. The only way this could work was if I drove to the commercial dental lab by 5 a.m., picked up his appliance and cemented it before 7 a.m. We were successful and Ed was very appreciative. I always tried to go the extra mile for the veterans. They deserved nothing less than that.

Ed Seward always loved to play golf and encouraged me to try the game on many occasions. When I finally expressed some interest he told me he had just replaced his driver and would bring in the old one for me to practice with.

I said, "Fine."

A few weeks later, Ed arrived late for his appointment but proudly held that driver in hand. He said he had forgotten the club and had to return home for it.

Knowing that his trip was nearly twenty five miles each way I said, "Ed, why did you go all the way back home to get that club for me?"

Ed smiled and replied, "Doc, I know you would do the same for me."

Ed Seward is now in his nineties and can no longer move as fast as he could during his youth but, after serving his country for most of his adult life, he deserves to take it easy now. I personally have known Ed for many years as both this dentist and his friend. For me it has been an honor to know and serve someone who has given so much for his country.

Ed after joining the Army Air Corps in WWII

Ed Seward's POW photograph

Damaged Messerschmitt factory from one of Ed's missions.

Ed Seward after retirement.

A PITCHER – EARL FULLER

I attended a funeral this past summer of a friend who taught me much about fishing and appreciating one's blessings. We first met nearly fifteen years ago while I was providing dental care to his closest friend "Smokey". Earl Fuller would accompany his fishing buddy for these visits and talk "fishing" with me before and after each visit. They had been friends since the war and had in fact both been captured on Corregidor, in the Philippines during the early days of World War II.

Several years later, Smokey passed away and Earl decided that I would now finally become his dentist and, a bit later, his fishing buddy. He taught me a very old technique and I soon perfected the skill of catching lake trout in New York's Finger Lakes. It was while on these trips that Earl would open up and share some of his dreadful war experiences.

One morning I asked, "How far is it from the Bataan Peninsula to Corregidor?"

"About as far as this lake is wide," was his reply. "By the time the Japanese were done shelling the island, there were hardly any trees left standing." And with these comments, Earl began his story.

Earl grew up in Springville, New York, and as a youngster would journey to Seneca Lake to fish with his uncle. His responsibility was to smack each fish on the head to dispatch it quickly. He enjoyed catching trout from the small row boat and knew that he would return there when he was grown. Earl also thought about becoming a soldier someday and was sure he would be a good one. Baseball was also a favorite of his and after high school, he pitched for a town team in Erie County.

In February of 1941, months before the war actually began, Earl enlisted in the army.

He was trained to repair and tie transmission antennas to frequency for communication and was assigned to the 10th Signal Corps of the 31st Infantry Division. His first choice was to go to the Philippine Islands in the Pacific. Little did he know what was about to take place in this region of the world. General Douglas MacArthur had recently been appointed by President Roosevelt to be the Allied Commander in the Philippines. He was assigned the responsibility of developing plans for the defense of the Philippine Islands.

When Pearl Harbor was attacked, MacArthur thought he would have some time before the Philippines might also be attacked but he was wrong. Japanese photo reconnaissance planes previously had located United States plane concentrations in the area. On December 8th, 1941, (December 7th Pearl Harbor time), the Japanese attacked and destroyed much of the US Army Air Corp installation in the Philippines. Now the Japanese forces were free to attack Manila which had been considered to be the finest harbor under United States flag in the western Pacific.

Earl had been sent with three other men to Fort McDowell about 25 miles away to set up some antennas. The men could hear the rumble of the explosions in the distance but were unsure what was happening. Upon returning, they discovered a notice saying that they should "leave as soon as possible." Most of his company had already left for Bataan but now the roads were closed. Earl was lucky enough to get on a ship bound for Corregidor along with Generals MacArthur, Sutherland, and other military personnel. Of the nearly 130,000 soldiers on the Philippine Islands at that time, most were Filipino and not yet combat ready.

Life on Corregidor was considerably different for Earl and the other men. They were on an island three miles from the tip of the Bataan peninsula. The tadpole shaped island was four miles long and one mile wide at its widest point. It had long been the site of a permanent garrison manned by costal artillery to repel a naval attack. Most of the Japanese forces were battling the men who had withdrawn to Bataan but some shelling was beginning on the island too. People who were there described three levels on the island. The highest portion was called "topside" and this was where the barracks and parade ground were located. The middle housed the hospital and the bottom had an elaborate tunnel system. The Malenta tunnel was 1,400 feet long and thirty feet wide. There were many lateral tunnels where supplies, ammunition, communications and headquarters were located.

Earl smiled when he told me of an unusual experience that occurred one night while he slept on his cot outside. "I saw something run by and thought it was a small deer but was certain I was dreaming. I asked the others the next morning and the said that it was Daisy the deer. She came every night after dark and slept in one of the bunks."

Earl was privileged to work directly with General MacArthur topside where he would operate a radio telephone. At 6 p.m. MacArthur would arrive and speak with the constabulary in Manila to find out how the war was progressing. They sat side by side. Earl would always stand up to salute but MacArthur would tell him to "stay seated soldier".

It was very near Christmas that the air raid sirens began to wail as the first real attack on the island commenced. Many of the men including MacArthur and Sutherland, the Chief of Staff, were caught out on the parade ground. Major General Sutherland was scared to death and ran for cover along with Earl. But not General Macarthur, he stood his ground. He was a very brave man and set a good example for the rest of the men according to Earl. The first plane dropped a bomb within fifty yards of the general. Sutherland who was hiding said, "Is the general still ok?'

MacArthur called for a staff car for his wife, son, and Chinese maid. He waited for a second car and took that to the bottom side. Earl always respected the general. "He treated me like a human being".

The attack continued and Earl ran to a machine gun nest only to find that both of the men there were already dead. He continued down the road to middle side until the road was strafed by another plane killing many Filipinos also attempting to escape.

In January, General McArthur sent a message to the troops on Bataan and Corregidor stating that help was on the way and that they should continue to fight bravely. This help never materialized for a number of reasons.

The air assaults continued on "The Rock" as it was also known and in February, shelling by artillery began as well. On March 11, General McArthur, his wife, son, Chinese maid and several others were evacuated from the island. During the next few months the attacks were sporadic until Bataan fell in April 9, 1942. Seventy six thousand men surrendered, mostly Filipinos, in what was considered the greatest defeat for Americans in history. It was discovered later that these men were subjected to brutal treatment by their captors with thousands dying during the "Bataan Death March".

General MacArthur and Earl actually shared the same birthday. For years after the war ended Earl received a birthday greeting from the General. I recall having a chill as I held and read one of those letters while interviewing my friend.

Earl was continually repairing the transmission lines destroyed by the explosions. One day the Major ordered him to do such a repair and asked. "How much time will you need?"

Earl stated confidently, "About twenty minutes should do."

Earl grabbed a coil of wire, climbed the hill and began working. While still holding the spliced wires in his hands 15 minutes later, the power was turned on. The jolt of electricity was so great he almost could not drop the wires. He ran back to the other men and said, "Who's the wise SOB that turned that power back on? I had 5 more minutes."

The major had. Earl was "busted" from corporal down to private for the remark.

On April 10, 1942, continuous shelling and bombing of the island began. One by one the coastal batteries were destroyed and the casualties began to mount. The effect a prolonged artillery attack has on anyone is profound. Any loud noise can elicit a response. As I was talking to Earl one day, a loud clap of thunder outside caused Earl to jump up from the kitchen table and look around. He said softly. "I'm sorry, Doc."

One day as his friend, Winters, and Earl were about to eat a fresh loaf of bread outside of Malenta tunnel, he had a strange idea something was about to happen. He said, "Run!" Almost immediately a 240 mm shell hit the exact place where they had been seated. Twenty-six other men were killed. Earl recalls a handsome MP walking around in obvious shock asking for help to put his severed arm back on. He died shortly afterward. Throughout these assaults, Earl continued to replace transmission lines until there were nearly no trees left to support them. For his dedication, he would later receive both the Bronze and Silver Stars for heroism.

On April 29, 1942, the birthday of the emperor of Japan, ten thousand shells smashed and raked the small island. During May 4th, sixteen thousand shells landed on what would be the final blow to "The Rock". By the next day the island was "broken, bare and naked" with only a few tree stumps remaining. That night the invasion began when thousands of Japanese troops came ashore. The fighting continued until there was no more to give and General Wainwright was forced to surrender. The date was May 6, 1942, and at 4:15 p.m. the War Department received a message from Corregidor stating that "resistance of our troops had been overcome and that fighting had ceased." Earl had wanted to be a good soldier and it hurt for him to see this finally occur.

The Japanese took everything the Americans had including their watches and rings. When there was nothing else of value, they would slap the prisoners. Two officers had graduated from West Point and were wearing their class rings. The Japanese noticed the rings and told the two men to give them up immediately. One refused and his finger with the ring was chopped off. The second officer complied immediately.

For the next month the men were held at the 92nd garage on the island. Several prisoners one day asked the guards if they could wade into the water to bathe and were given permission. As the group entered the water, however, the guards opened up with a machine gun and shot all of them. Surrender was considered humiliation for the Japanese who would rather die first. This may explain the brutality that the Americans were subjected to by their captors.

The prisoners were taken by boat back to the Old Bilibad Prison in Manila on Decoration Day. The stars and stripes that had flown in Manila had been replaced by Japanese flags. It was here that some of the worst experiences of his life occurred.

The prisoners had been told to always bow to the Japanese officers as a sign of respect. Earl was standing with some other men and the man right next to him had a momentary memory lapse and did not bow when the others did. This was an unforgiveable offense and his head was promptly removed with one swing of the officer's sword.

Earl also witnessed a Filipino civilian attempt to throw some rice to the prisoners. The guard attacked this person and slashed his throat.

After one month, they were transported by train for one day and then marched for two more until they reached their new destination, the dreaded Cabanatuan Camp. It was now the rainy season so the journey had been very difficult. Food now consisted of a rice ball the size of a baseball and a cup of tea per day. The latrine was on a slippery slope and the men often slid into the mess as they tried to defecate. They had to be rescued by the other prisoners when this happened. Because of the malnutrition and poor sanitation they experienced, Earl and many other men became ill with diseases such as tuberculosis, dysentery, and malaria during their confinement.

One prisoner was very sick with malaria and unable to leave the hut. A worker came one day to repair the roof and the prisoner stole his food. Fearing he would be severely punished, he took the food to the latrine and buried it. The worker reported this incident to the guards. The prisoners were gathered together and the guard demanded that the person who stole the food step forward. Nobody moved initially. They were told they would stand there until the thief confessed. Finally the guy stepped forward.

"Where is the food?" they demanded.

"In the latrine." he replied.

"Go get it. "They ordered.

Once he retrieved the food now covered with feces, they ordered. "Eat it."

As he tried to do so he began to vomit.

The guards then locked this prisoner in a guard house and began jabbing him with pointed bamboo poles. Eventually he died.

The guards did allow them to catch a stray dog one day and all but two of the prisoners ate the soup that was prepared from it.

One evening an ill naked man was backing down the steps to use the latrine but could not hold it any longer. Open boxes of rice nearby were spattered. The following day, the men ate their ration of rice from the boxes, in spite of the feces. It is not surprising that nearly forty percent of the prisoners died during captivity.

The surviving prisoners were transported by ship to Japan. During their trip, Earl remembers his ship being fired upon by a surfaced Allied submarine. The ship directly behind Earl's was hit twice and, if not for the escorting Japanese destroyer, some of the vessels may have been sunk. Once they arrived in Japan, one Japanese officer said they should "be thankful for the life preservers the emperor had provided during the attack."

He soon realized that survival might depend on his learning to speak Japanese. There was one guard known as Kinnisha San who had been wounded in Singapore and seemed interested in learning English. Earl would speak with him regularly. This relationship would prove to be of value now that they had reached Japan, his home for the next three years.

The guard told him that Babe Ruth had once come to Japan and that baseball was popular there. Earl was asked what position he played and Earl replied that he was a pitcher. Kinnisha San spoke to his commanding officer who suggested that the prisoners play against the Japanese. Earl said they were in no condition to play ball and had no equipment. Gloves were soon provided and they were told they had one week to practice. He was also told privately that under no circumstances were the prisoners to win.

The game was scheduled to be played on Sunday and the people from the villages would be invited to attend. Because of their poor physical condition, the game would last only five innings. Earl would be pitching for the team of POWs. His friend Gregory from Brooklyn would catch and he also understood but did not like the arrangements Earl had made. The game was tied in the last inning and the Japanese had a man on base. The Japanese commander came up to bat and he was a very good ball player. Earl called Greg to the mound and told him he was going to put one right down the middle. Earl can still to this day see that ball going. He hit it a mile and the Japanese won the game.

Earl's team mates knew he had thrown the game and said he was a disgrace. He took a lot of abuse until the next day when an ox drawn cart carrying thousands of tangerines arrived for the prisoners. The following day a second cart loaded with small fish was delivered again for the men. The fish lasted for three days. This was the first food other than rice that they had had in many months. The other men soon realized what Earl had done for them. Not only had the respect they had earned from their opponents on the ball field resulted in this food but Earl had probably also saved their lives.

Time passed and the men were moved from one camp to another where they were required to work daily. Earl's elbow was seriously injured moving carts loaded with stone in Tanagwa. The injury would bother him the rest of his life.

One day, United States Navy planes strafed the area near their camp. "The planes were only about 300 feet above us," Earl recalls. The prisoners waved frantically at the planes. They were hoping to be seen but received no sign of acknowledgement from the occupants of the aircraft that they had been noticed.

By the time they had reached the last prison camp, Saruga, the brutal treatment by their captors had lessened. For the first time they were given Red Cross parcels containing food. Now, if they could only survive the more frequent Allied attacks on mainland Japan was the question. The prisoners also understood that if an invasion took place they would all probably be executed.

The strafing and bombing of Japan and their prison camp continued until one day, Kinnisha San told Earl to "run into the mountains". Orders to execute the prisoners were not carried out fortunately. As Earl ran past his former adversary and friend he stopped and they saluted each other. He would never see this man again. If not for Kinnisha San, Earl would not have escaped or survived.

General Homma, who was considered to be responsible for the "Bataan Death March" and brutalization of the captives, was executed by firing squad in Manila on April 3, 1946.

Earl Fuller would return to the United States a free man and settle on the shores of Seneca Lake in Upstate New York. This is where we would fish together years later - probing the lake's depths in search of lake trout.

Earl did not use a fishing pole but instead a very old windup record played or Victrola, as it was known. The turntable had been replaced with

MY HEROES AND THEIR STORIES OF SURVIVAL

a large spool. This contained a few hundred yards of fine copper wire to which a lure was attached. As this was trolled over the lake's bottom, one could actually feel the rocks until, that is, one of those trout grabbed ahold. Once landed the fish was treated with his small bat shaped club to "quiet it down."

One day when we were done fishing, he handed me one of his two prized fishing Victrolas. "Here Doc, now you know how it's done, go catch some fish."

Today when I load his old Victrola spooled with copper wire into my boat, along with the lures he taught me to make, I sense his presence. I can still see him sitting at the rear of his boat working his magic. Earl would look around at the water, smile and say, "Boy, Doc! What a beautiful day!"

When I think of the deprivation and brutality this man endured during his ordeal and the appreciation for life that he demonstrated, I realize that I am very fortunate to have known this man and called him my friend. He is an inspiration to me and would be for anyone who knew him.

Earl as a young GI and member of the Signal Corps.

Photo of Japanese prison guards including the one who
befriended him, front row second from left.

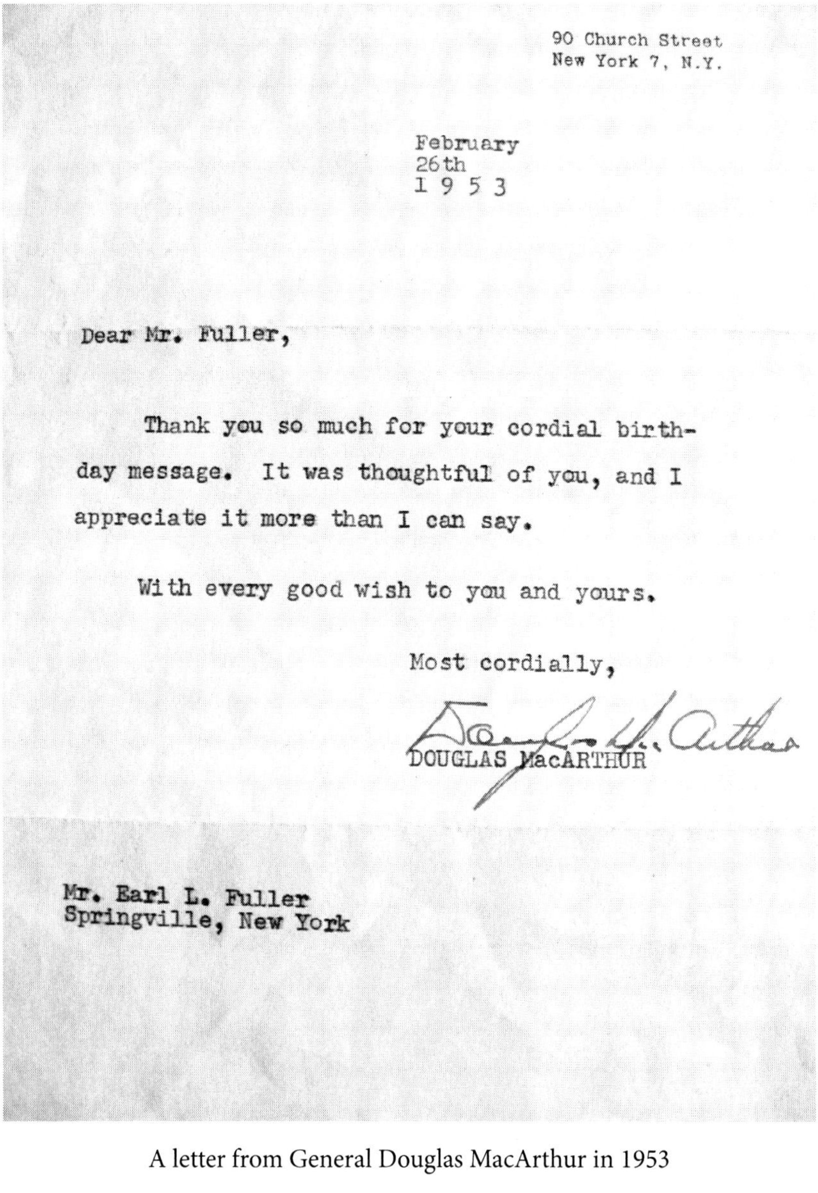

90 Church Street
New York 7, N.Y.

February
26th
1 9 5 3

Dear Mr. Fuller,

Thank you so much for your cordial birthday message. It was thoughtful of you, and I
appreciate it more than I can say.

With every good wish to you and yours.

Most cordially,

DOUGLAS MacARTHUR

Mr. Earl L. Fuller
Springville, New York

A letter from General Douglas MacArthur in 1953

Earl with the "Doc" after a fishing trip

IT WAS HELL! —ANTHONY VISCO

George was playing his harmonica and the other boys were singing along as their glider lumbered slowly behind the C-47 crossing the English Channel. As they neared the Normandy beaches, the men noticed the pilot putting his flak jacket on. Peering out into the haze, they saw explosions everywhere around the plane. Red thought, "Holy shit!" as the men suddenly got very quiet. "We're done for!"

For Anthony "Red" Visco, this was a far cry from the simple life he was accustomed to back home. Born January 13, 1921, in Geneva, New York, Red had grown up enjoying hunting and fishing. He left school after the eighth grade and began working. After all, most Americans were suffering during the depression. Everyone needed to pitch in.

When war broke out in Europe and the Pacific, Anthony wanted to volunteer but his father would not consent. He waited until he was 21, and then joined the United States Army. After a brief stay at Fort Niagara in upstate New York, it was off to Fort Bragg, North Carolina. Anthony was earning $69 a month at this point but when he heard of a new division forming with more pay he decided to go for it. Now he would be receiving $50 more each month as a member of the 101st Airborne Division.

At first, the training was very strenuous but soon he became accustomed to the new routine. It seemed that they had to run everywhere. "We ran to chow, we even ran to the church!" Anthony remembers one forced march of 25 miles carrying a full pack. This extra conditioning, however, helped prepare him for what would follow.

In the fall of 1943 the new 101st Airborne Division was transported to England by ship and was initially based in Reading near London where the men lived in barracks. The 82nd Airborne Division had just returned from combat in Italy and was in need of replacements. The entire third Battalion of the 101st was transferred to the 82nd Airborne Division. Now the men lived in tents but continued to train for their upcoming mission.

Anthony fondly remembers an older British lady who, along with her husband, ran a cafeteria nearby. In a sense she adopted him and had him over every day for tea, a beverage he continues to enjoy today. After the war, he remained in contact with this lady and her husband until they both had passed away.

Anthony shared his story with me eventually but usually preferred to talk about either hunting or fishing when he came for his dental appointments. Naturally, I had to share a few of my own stories with him. Describing a recent pheasant hunting trip my son and I had taken to South Dakota really put a smile on his face. He just could not believe how great the hunting had been on that trip.

At one of his visits, I remember Red telling me how many pheasants there were in this area years ago. He paused and said, "Doc, were there really that many pheasants in South Dakota?"

I said, "Wait a minute!" and produced a photograph that I had in my office. The picture had been taken in a three stall garage where hunters brought the birds they had bagged for processing very similar to operations I was familiar with where deer are butchered. Each hunter could bring his limit of three pheasants per day. While the periphery of the garage was lined with several freezers what was astonishing was the day's take of birds on the floor. They were piled nearly a foot deep. There was more than a thousand pheasants yet to be cleaned from that day. When Red saw this his eyes got huge and he repeated his favorite comment, "Holy Shit Doc!"

The journey across the English Channel on D-Day did not take place in the small glider he had trained with in the states. There the pilot was so good he could actually land the glider on a handkerchief in the middle of a field. The Horsa glider was much larger and clumsy. In spite of the German flak that had filled the sky, the glider managed to crash land between two hedgerows that were common in this part of France. At first, the men simply wanted to run in a certain direction but Anthony remembered their orders to wait for the radioman. Finally the radioman arrived and he knew where they needed to go. Anthony remembers that they were already surrounded by the Germans.

Soon they encountered a German 88 and several machine guns hidden in a hedgerow. The deadly 88 artillery piece Anthony recalls was like a bolt of lightning; by the time you heard it go off it was already too late. They managed to take out the machine guns and eventually got the 88 also.

The troops slowly made their way towards St. Marie Eglise but soon came to a heavily fortified bridge. The Germans had it zeroed in with their very powerful machine guns. The bridge was about 30 feet wide and they absolutely had to make it across. They succeeded but lost a lot of men doing so. Anthony paused during this portion of his story and said, "It was like a bad dream."

Early that afternoon, his unit captured a German soldier who, when interviewed, said that they were planning a counterattack at 4 p.m. Upon learning this, the general told the Americans to load up with ammo, grenades and fix their bayonets. When the screaming Americans attacked the organizing enemy units the Germans surprisingly began running away. Many of them simply did not want to fight any longer.

Soon the men of the 82nd were relieved by another division. The men needed a break but this was short-lived. The new units were firing ammunition with tracers that immediately gave their position away. They were quickly attacked and routed by the German Luftwaffe. Anthony's unit needed to return to the front lines when this occurred.

The Americans were now moving very slowly from hedgerow to hedgerow but running low on ammunition. The pontoon bridges that the

Americans constructed across the rivers were blown up by the Germans to delay the advancing Allied forces.

By this time, the 82nd division needed replacements due to the heavy losses sustained and the men were allowed to recover for a while. In early September they were again boarding gliders for another significant battle in Holland, later known as Operation Market Garden. This time Anthony remembers the glider landing smoothly in a large field that was actually a cow pasture. After some fighting, the Americans found themselves surrounded by the Germans. They fought on however in spite of this. Red remembers that some of the civilians would help feed the men occasionally. They appreciated this after living on both C and K rations during combat.

Again the 82nd was relieved and allowed to return to Paris to recover from the strain of battle. By this time, Anthony and many of the men had already accumulated enough points that they could be sent home. Things quickly changed and their passes were canceled. The men boarded trucks but were not heading home. Instead they were heading north to Belgium where the Germans were counterattacking. They left so quickly that the men of the 82nd were still wearing their lighter summer clothes, regular G.I. boots and no gloves. They were not prepared, unfortunately, for their next battle later referred to as the Battle of the Bulge.

Anthony remembers fighting for days on end under frigid conditions. Many of the men suffered frozen feet but Anthony was fortunate that this did not happen to him. When they tried to get some "shut eye", they would wake up covered with snow. It was here that one of his horrible memories took place. Anthony remembers American bodies lying everywhere in the snow and tanks driving right over the corpses. I remember Anthony pausing and wiping his eyes as he shared this incident with me.

Around Christmas men were notified that they were going to have a hot meal. Anthony remembers that the men were sitting on a hill when the containers with hot chicken arrived. It had been cloudy for several days so that the Allied Air Force had been unable to support the men in combat.

As they opened the containers and began eating their hot meal, they heard the grinding sound of metal in the distance. A column of German tanks appeared on the road and was heading in their direction. Just when it appeared that their meal was over, the clouds parted and Allied fighter planes swooped down on the enemy tanks. As Anthony recalls, "They knocked the shit out of them. All we had to do was watch the action and enjoy our hot meal."

For the next several weeks, the 82nd division was on the move but with much less resistance from the Germans who were retreating deeper into Germany. It was at this time that the Allied forces began to discover some of the Nazi atrocities, the concentration camps. Anthony remembers one man they found from Greece that was "all skin and bones".

Once the Allies reached Berlin and the war ended, the 82nd became part of a large occupation force in Germany. Anthony remembers being very near the Russians who he felt were very crude. They would take anything they wanted and when they were drunk would shoot their guns indiscriminately. A few GIs were hit accidentally by the rowdy Russians. His only humorous memory of being in Berlin was when they shared the Russians' vodka. "It was so strong we had to cut it with orange juice."

After returning home and being discharged, Anthony worked briefly at the Seneca Army depot before beginning a long career working as a baker. He enjoyed this type of work especially when he worked at Hobart College and had more time to fish and hunt.

I remember Anthony pausing as he thought back about his experiences in the war and finally said, "People in our country don't know what hell is. They have never had to suffer."

Red passed away a few months after sharing his memories with me. As I prepared to leave his home on what would be our last visit he said, "Doc there are still a lot of bad dreams." And then he began to wipe his eyes saying softly, "It is great to live in America, people do not realize how lucky they are to be free."

Anthony holding a photograph about D-day.

A BIBLE -- LES CONOVER

The soldiers had been convalescing in England for several
months and just had to get out of the hospital for a while. After discussing
several options, the five men clad in pajamas and bathrobes slipped out
and slowly made their way to a nearby pub. The cold beer looked so good
but before a drop could be swallowed, the door flew open and two officers
entered. "What are you guys doing here?" they shouted. Down went the
glasses and the enlisted men slowly exited the tavern.

One of the five was a young man named Les Conover. He had been
born in 1918 and raised on a farm in upstate New York. Like many boys
of that era, he loved to hunt and fish. After graduating from high school in
1938, he went to work for Bausch & Lomb Company. There he worked on
equipment, such as binoculars, that was being made for the United States
Navy for the war. Les actually received several deferments from the military because of this important work. In September of 1944, however, his
life changed when he was drafted. After completing basic training, he was
sent to Europe at a time when it appeared that Germany was nearly beaten.
Unfortunately, Hitler had plans for a great offensive that he hoped would
change the course of the war, what would later be known as the Battle of
the Bulge.

Just before departing, Les was given a small Bible by his dad and told
to, "keep it near your heart and read a verse every day."

Unfortunately, when Les found himself in the cold forests of Belgium during the ferocious attack by the Germans, he rarely had time to comply with his father's wishes. The Bible, however, was always with him.

With mortar shells exploding all around, the Americans still managed to capture two German soldiers. Les, however, was wounded seriously by the shrapnel. These two prisoners had obviously had enough fighting and did not try to escape. Instead they lifted the wounded American to his feet. With one arm draped over the shoulder of each German, Les was slowly dragged across a field roughly 1000 feet to where the medics were located. In combat, one man usually tries to kill the other but when faced with an injured human being, they sometimes are compassionate. With the heavy loss of blood and freezing temperature, Les was shivering uncontrollably. This prompted one of the Germans to remove his wool gloves and place them on the injured American's hands. As the three men made their way across the field, a German machine gun opened fire hitting all around them but missing the three soldiers. They seemed reluctant to hit one of their own men to kill the GI.

Once in the woods, Les began receiving first aid. He was placed on a stretcher and loaded onto a jeep. He recalls having surgery in Luxembourg and again in England to remove shrapnel from his legs and back very near his spine. Eventually the young soldier recovered enough for that escapade at the local pub before returning to the United States.

Les was always used to hard manual labor and transitioning to carpentry work, building and remodeling homes, was easy as a civilian. Now in his 90's he still looks physically fit. One of my other patients recently asked, "How old is that veteran?"

When I answered he could not believe it and stated, "He looks like he could still do pushups."

I will never forget my interview with Les Conover. He arrived carrying a small box. After recording his combat experiences during World War II, I finally had to ask him what he had brought in the box. Les slowly opened it and removed a pair of wool gloves, stained with his dried blood and handed them to me. I was speechless and had goosebumps.

Next he removed a small Bible with an inscription inside the cover that read. "Son, keep this close to your heart and God will always protect you."

Signed "Your Dad."

I asked if the advice helped him survive.

He replied emphatically, "Absolutely, the Bible saved me."

Young Les shortly after joining the Army.

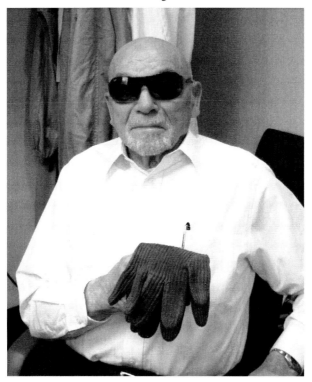

The Bible and message from his father.

Les holding the wool gloves from the captured German.

THE TOGGLIER -- FRED FLETCHER

As he fell from his plane, Fred pulled on what he thought was his parachute rip cord but nothing happened. He pulled again and nothing. Suddenly he realized he was pulling the carrying handle instead. Quickly he grabbed the real ripcord but the chute still would not open. Fred did not have much time left. Would this be the end? Finally, when he realized that he was gripping the parachute so tightly against his chest that it could not deploy, Fred released his hold and the chute opened. He could hear shouting from below and then shots rang out. These were shots aimed at him and his crew members.

Fred Fletcher had been born in West Virginia in 1924. At five years of age, his family moved to Utica, Michigan, for his father's new job, pumping oil across the border into Canada. The work was steady even though the depression had started. After graduating from high school, he assumed that he would be drafted since the war was already raging in both Europe and the Pacific. Fred volunteered for training as a navy pilot but was rejected because of problems with his teeth. He joined the Army and was assigned to the Air Force.

After completing basic training, he was sent to Armorer School in Colorado and then on to Aerial Gunner School in Texas. Fred joined a B-17 crew and completed three more months of training with this group of young men. In Savannah, Georgia, they picked up a new airplane and flew to New Hampshire. The crew then flew across the Atlantic Ocean and eventually ended up in Deenethorpe, England, the home of the 401st Bomb Group. They were now a part of the mighty 8th Air Force

During World War II there was the 8th, 9th and 15th Air Force based in Europe. The 8th consisted of four engine heavy bombers both B-17s and B-24s and smaller fighter planes. The 9th Air Force consisted of medium bombers such as B-26s, B-25s and also various fighter planes. Together these two forces were spread over 122 air bases in England. The symbol on the heavy bombers; a triangle, a square, or a circle indicated which division (1st, 2nd, 3rd) the plane was assigned to. The crew of the B-17 consisted of 10 men initially with a right and left waist gunner but later in the war, when the Luftwaffe had been depleted, one man was able to operate both of these machine guns. Fred Fletcher was responsible for the right waist defensive position.

Typically, after breakfast, the crew members were briefed on the mission and then taken to their plane by truck. The time for the briefing was determined by the distance to a given target. For example, on Fred's last mission the crew boarded their bomber at 3:30 a.m. and prepared for take-off. At 4:30 a.m. the engines started and by 4:45 a.m. the planes began to taxi towards the runway. At 4:55 a.m. these bombers began to take off. By the time all the planes were in the air and properly organized for the mission, it was nearly 6:30 in the morning.

Initially Fred's crew was assigned to fly in a B-17 F known as "Duffy's Tavern". This plane had an open waist gun position on the side, but no chin turret up front. After completing several missions, they received a newer model for their D-Day mission. The pilot, Lieutenant McKeon, named the plane with his wife's nickname "D-Day Dottie". The bombardier, Lieutenant Koslowski had been killed on the July 6 mission and Fred was promoted to this new position with the designation of "Togglier/Bombardier". Fred would now be responsible for operating the chin gun turret, the bomb bay controls, and the toggle switch that released the plane's bombs. Once the lead plane with a bomb sight released their bomb load, Fred and the other planes would follow.

July 19, 1944, is the date that Fred Fletcher will never forget. The target for his wing of 123 bombers on that clear summer day was Augsburg, Germany. Their plane was being repaired so they were assigned a replacement for that mission. A total of 1080 bombers and 761 fighter planes flew in a formation nearly 150 miles long on that morning into southwestern Germany. After dropping their bombs on the Messerschmitt factory, Fred's plane was hit by enemy flak as they flew over Stuttgart, Germany. One engine was knocked out but the pilot immediately feathered it to prevent wind milling and drag from the disabled engine. (This means that the propeller is perpendicular to the direction of flight.) A second engine, also hit, could not be feathered. The supercharger on the third engine was blown so the aircraft was actually attempting to fly with only one and one half engines operating. The aircraft quickly lost altitude dropping from nearly 25,000 feet to approximately 10,000 feet forcing the pilot to have his crew discard all guns, ammunition and any other heavy objects to lighten his plane. The ball turret could not be released because the necessary tool was not available in the borrowed plane. Had the plane possessed full power, they could have easily crossed the mountains into neutral Switzerland. This was now impossible.

Fred is a technically oriented person with a knack for explaining in detail how mechanical devices operate. I clearly recall one day, while sitting in my dental chair, his description of how pilots controlled air speed by changing propeller pitch, RPM and engine fuel mixture for each of four engines on the B-17.

During takeoff, a rich gas mixture, high RPM and a prop pitch that would take a "low bite" was necessary. This was similar to low gear in an automobile according to Fred. Once cruising altitude was reached, the fuel mixture was leaner, the RPM less and the pitch took a "larger bite" of the air. What is remarkable to me is that the crew members of these bombers were not far removed from high school at this time.

Their aircraft gradually descended over the next three hours to approximately 800 feet above sea level or approximately 650 feet above the ground. They were flying west over France and down the Loire River valley. Initially the plan was to fly towards the Allied beachhead in Normandy, but they quickly decided to fly instead towards the Brest Peninsula, a much safer route and ditch the plane at sea. As the aircraft limped along at less than 100 miles an hour they were actually an inviting target for enemy soldiers below. Anti-aircraft fired at the plane only succeeded in blowing large holes in the wings since the fuses were set for much higher targets. With the plane so riddled from the shooting, with little power and damaged cables, it would only fly with the tail lower than the fuselage. Frederick recalls this being a long and frightening experience. After being shot at for more than 3 hours suddenly two Me109s appeared on the left of their crippled aircraft and lowered their landing gear, most likely a signal for the Americans to land and surrender. They were near Anjou, France.

Years later Fred stated that the "area was known for fine wines" but at that time all he noticed was that virtually every bridge over the river had been destroyed by Allied bombing. The objective was to make it difficult for the German army to move troops and supplies.

The pilot gave the order to bail out but he and the copilot remained onboard with the plane, now on autopilot, a while longer. Fred was the second to exit the plane but unfortunately his parachute would not open. After several attempts he finally succeeded and hit the ground within 20 seconds of the chute opening. He had landed on a German airfield.

Voices could soon be heard from approaching German soldiers. They wore the blue trousers of the Luftwaffe and quickly captured Fred. Jack, the radio operator, landed nearby and pointed out three Me 109s hidden under trees nearby. The pilot and copilot continued on with the plane until being attacked by more enemy fighters forcing them to also bail out. Since the plane was still flying on autopilot when they jumped out, it continued on but flying in a circular route. The damaged tail rudder was fixed in position. About 15 minutes later, Fred's German captors became excited as his tail dragging B-17 came lumbering back towards them. It finally stalled out and crashed 2 km away.

In early 2000, Fred Fletcher received a lengthy letter from a gentleman named Pierre in France. He had been doing a research project investigating "crash sites" from WWII. There were actually witnesses still alive that remember the plane flying very low over the town and crashing. He had obtained copies of photographs with German soldiers posing next to Fred's plane at the crash site. Damage sustained to the tail section in flight was clearly evident.

The prisoners were taken to a château for interrogation where Colonel Reorder of the Luftwaffe had his office and sleeping quarters. Werner Zukunft, the navigator, had been born in Germany but never revealed to the captors that he understood everything they were saying about the prisoners. The officer was very angry with him and could not understand how a man with a good German name like his could bomb the fatherland. Fred discovered later that all nine members of his crew had survived on this mission where 18 planes had been shot down and another 367 damaged. Of the planes downed by the Germans, eleven were B-17s.

It is really ironic that another patient of mine was the bombardier on one of the eleven that was lost on that particular mission. The two veterans discovered this when they met after moving into the same retirement community a few years ago.

They were next held in the building that had been part of a French flying school. The group was soon joined by two other American flyers one of whom was a P-38 pilot. His name was Lieutenant Gerald Hart and he was wearing only his shoes, socks and trousers when he arrived. Fred remembers that he had a tanned and well-muscled body. This was strange to the crew of the bombers that had flown only in cold aircraft. They had to wear electric flying suits inside to tolerate the -30 degree temperature at 28,000 feet. Apparently Lieutenant Hart had been playing baseball back in England when the order came to go on a mission. With a heated cockpit, heavy clothing was not necessary at least for Hart.

He was very cocky and bragged that he could hit a 1 meter target 150 times out of 200 shots with machine guns on his P-38. This plane had two engines situated on either side of a "pod" containing the pilot. There was nothing to distract the pilot when he was firing the machine guns located on that pod. On that day however he had made a fatal mistake of attacking an enemy target and making a second pass. This time he had been shot down.

Later when one of the guards commented that the German men were the best fighters in the world, Lieutenant Hart immediately challenged him to a fist fight. The German would not accept this offer and backed down.

The prisoners were transported at night in a truck with German guards and a French mechanic. The mechanic came in handy repairing several flat tires. These were caused by boards with protruding nails that had been strewn on the roads by the French underground. The prisoners were eventually taken to Frankfurt, Germany, for interrogation and Dulag Luft near Wentzler. Here they were reunited with the other members of their crew during the eight day stay before continuing on to a prison camp.

Of the more than 130,000 American prisoners in World War II, 94,000 were captured in Europe and most were airmen.

Normally officers and enlisted men were separated and sent to different prison camps. Fred volunteered to be sent to one of the officer's camps where he could work possibly as an orderly and clean the rooms. He thought this would be better than to stay with other enlisted men where there might be more confusion and worse living conditions since they would be enlisted men of similar rank. He got his wish and was transferred to Stamlager III (Stalag Luft III) near Sagan, Poland.

Fred was assigned to the North Compound which housed primarily British officers. They did not realize it at the time but their POW camp was only a few miles from a concentration camp known as Auschwitz. He arrived at his new home on August 12, 1944, and joined 15,000 other prisoners in five compounds being held there. They were mostly American and British airmen but there was also a Russian prisoner work camp nearby. Fred remembers having his wristwatch taken from him but receiving a receipt for this transaction. He still has the receipt but never received his watch back. Prior to his arrival the "Great Escape" had been attempted at this prison camp by British airmen who had been there for years.

The men survived for the nearly 5 months in this prison camp depending on Red Cross parcels mainly. The captives were awakened one night in January, 1945, and told they must prepare to leave taking with them only what they could carry. The Russians were advancing from the East. Wearing only a medium weight RAF winter coat and GI shoes, Fred began his journey during a blizzard. The captives had constructed sleds out of bed slats and were dragging their Red Cross parcels through the snow. It was very cold. For a while they walked along the autobahn that was empty of vehicles at the time. German citizens, however, were also walking west also trying to stay ahead of the advancing Russians. They had obviously endured much hardship during the war too. The first two nights they were allowed to sleep in barns along the road. After a while the rain began and the sleds had to be discarded.

Fred remembers the British airmen always finding ways to have their tea. He even once witnessed them boiling snow to make tea.

After walking four days and covering nearly 50 miles, they finally boarded boxcars of a train and were taken to Nuremberg and Stalag 13d. They arrived on February 3, 1945. The Allied soldiers recently captured in the historic Battle of the Bulge were also being sent there in large numbers. Fred claims that this was the most depressing place he has ever been. This camp was filthy and congested. Food from the Red Cross parcels was no longer available and their captors provided little for so many starving prisoners. Having "too little heat and not much food was the worst part of being a prisoner."

About this time, Allied forces became aware that prisoners were being forced to march long distances in horrible weather and promptly notified Germany that this had to stop. It was considered a war crime for them to continue such harsh treatment of prisoners.

In March, 1945, white G.I. trucks operated by the Swiss Red Cross were allowed to enter Germany from Switzerland carrying badly needed Red Cross parcels for prisoners there. They were permitted to do so as long as the truck was driven by a Swiss driver, used only their own gasoline and were able to return on the same day. Only prisoner camps within the range of these trucks could have the supplies. Luckily, Stalag 13d was within this range.

By April the prisoners were again walking, this time to Moosburg near Munich and again were able to obtain some food from these trucks. Some of the prisoners even traded with local farmers for food. While this was happening, United States aircraft monitored the POW column. The weather had improved significantly by this time so their journey was not nearly as harsh. Moosburg had nearly 50,000 prisoners and many were from England and British colonies. The Germans had hoped to trade these prisoners eventually for better treatment once the war ended. After a short time in this wretched place, the war finally was over.

Fred returned to the United States and after a furlough was sent to Atlantic City. An announcement was made that any servicemen interested in attending college under the GI Bill should see the Sargent at the Convention Center. His first choice was to become an aeronautical engineer but already pages of names had been recorded for that. Instead he chose chemical engineering where there are only two names listed. The next question was what school he wanted to attend. His answer was MIT.

Fred claims that he was rather "cavalier" with both choices assuming neither would be granted. He was incorrect.

Soon a letter arrived from Cecelia Brickser, his girlfriend back home, who was training to become a nurse. Shortly thereafter they were married and a new life began for Fred. He completed college and helped his bride to raise seven children in the years to follow.

As to the question about Fred's dental problem that prevented him from becoming a pilot, it turned out that there really was no problem. As his dentist for the past 15 years I can attest to the fact that he still has most of his natural teeth remaining and that "the dental problem" never interfered with him enjoying life and his family after World War II.

Fred second from the left with the crew from his B 17

B-17G No. 44-6129 of the 401st Bomb Group shot down near Corné France 19 July 1944. Fred Fletcher was the bombardier. The Luftwaffe members shown in the photo are likely from JG-27.

Luftwaffe posing with the wreckage of Fred's plane.

Fred Fletcher with his wife Cecelia

DEUCE AND A HALF
-- LYLE CORLETT

Through the eerie darkness, Lyle was certain he could hear the unmistakable screeching rumble of armor over the soft hum of his truck's engine. Were they ours or theirs? On this road to Bastogne, he needed to be extremely cautious. He slowly backed the truck off the road and into a clearing in the heavy forest. The sounds grew louder and soon block out lights became visible, but larger than those he was accustomed to. The column of German halftracks and tanks might not detect him if his luck would hold out a bit longer.

As a boy growing up in Rochester, New York, Lyle Corlett had never been afraid of anything. After all, what was there to fear playing baseball? Yes, he was disappointed not to play on the varsity team at Madison High School but after "making a pest of myself", he was allowed to join the JV team as a senior. This wasn't so bad. Other children who had grown up in the Depression had had it much more difficult.

His first job after graduating from high school was in a stockbroker's office where he earned only six dollars per week. But Lyle missed high school so much that he returned for further studies as a PG or post graduate. After a brief stint back at school and another poor paying position in a jewelry store, he finally hit the big time working for Graflex. He could now afford to enjoy himself and even began dating some of the young ladies.

Lyle laughs when he remembers his first real date. "I took this young lady on a bus to see a baseball game and we froze from the cold. Afterwards, we went to a nice restaurant downtown where I, unfortunately, ordered first. I ordered a really big meal. She only ordered a sandwich. I was embarrassed. That was the last time I saw her."

His life changed when the United States entered the war and young Lyle was drafted into the Army. In March of 1943, he was sent to Fort Niagara in upstate New York where they slept in a poorly heated barracks. After a brief stay there, the young soldiers boarded a troop train bound for Oregon and three months of basic training. At first, he was homesick but realized that none of the other boys had ever been this far from home. The next phase of training, under combat conditions, was more intense. That fall he was sent to Fort Lewis, Washington, where more drilling took place. Pfc. Corlett felt like a real soldier when he arrived at Fort Pierce, Florida, and began training with the Navy for something called "amphibious landings". Things were happening fast for young Lyle and after a brief stay at Camp Pickett, Virginia, he was sent to New Jersey, the port of embarkation. It was now time for these young men to be shipped overseas.

When Lyle was in basic training, he had learned how to drive what was known as a 6 x 6 or two and a half-ton truck. Now that he was in England, the company he was assigned to was notified that they would be landing on the first wave of the invasion. Lyle discovered, however, that the drivers would remain behind. On June 6, 1944, Lyle was still in the camp in England but the rest of the company did not fare as well. Thirty of them were lost on D-Day including two of his friends from Rochester. Had he been fortunate or just plain lucky? Lyle said he has "thought back a thousand times over what happened. I had no control. Why them and not me?"

The 30 or 40 men who dealt with the motor vehicles finally joined their company eight days later when the fighting had moved inland nearly 2 miles. Once in France however, Lyle joined a unit of combat engineers, a special unit of infantrymen who could also build, repair and demolish roads and bridges when necessary.

After months of fighting, the Germans were being driven back and began to appear beaten. By November of 1944, Lyle was "holed up" in a monastery in northern France awaiting orders for their next assignment. Lyle remembers the night of December 16th vividly. He and a buddy had gone to town to enjoy the company of two young schoolteachers. Naturally the parents were present for this event and they enjoyed desserts together. They returned to camp at approximately 10 p.m. and went to sleep. Around 3 a.m., however, he was awakened by considerable noise and confusion. They were told that the Germans had "broken through" and told "get ready to move out."

By early morning the trucks had been loaded and the battalion began its journey north towards a city in Belgium known as Bastogne. After moving nearly 50 miles, the battalion halted and bivouacked in a nearby field. On the afternoon of the 18th, a second lieutenant notified Lyle and his buddy, another driver, that they should prepare to depart with two trucks loaded with troops and explosives. Their job was to demolish some of the bridges leading to Bastogne and halt the German advance. The enemy's objective, it was later discovered was to control the roads and bridges in this strategic city so they could quickly move men and supplies west towards the important port of Antwerp, Belgium.

Early in the evening of the 19th, they set out through the southern Ardennes but were moving very slowly with only "blackout lights." It was exceedingly dark and therefore very hard to navigate. Moving only a couple of miles took considerable time. Soon they came to an intersection guarded by MPs and a small tank. The truck stopped and a lieutenant from the other truck got out and proceeded to talk to these men. Lyle could only surmise that there was no bad news and they were allowed to move on. It was very cold, only in the 20s, and exceedingly dark. Near this intersection there was also what appeared to be a medical unit with many Red Cross trucks. They were clearly marked with red crosses from top to bottom and front to back.

The trucks proceeded slowly with the limited visibility until Lyle heard the sound of heavy armor approaching ahead. Suspecting the worst, the lieutenant directed them to get the trucks off the road. They noticed two clearings in the heavy forest bordering the road, one at either side. Each truck backed slowly into an opening and stopped nearly 60 feet off of the road. The soldiers in the rear of each truck dispersed into the woods but the drivers were told to remain with their trucks in case they were needed in a hurry. The screeching sound of the armor grew louder until Lyle could see the blackout lights approaching one to two hundred feet to his left. These lights were much larger, definitely not American. "They're Germans." With such poor visibility he hoped that his luck could hold out once more, and he would not be discovered.

Three or four German halftracks moved slowly past his hiding spot when suddenly a German hollered loudly and the column stopped. A blinding searchlight nearly 3 feet in diameter slowly rotated in his direction and stopped on Lyle's truck. He could make out the form of a man approaching, a German officer brandishing a Lugar. Terrified Lyle thought "Don't move a muscle or you're gone." He was hardly breathing when the officer motioned for him to get out of the truck and drop his sidearm. Lyle began to think that this must all be a bad dream. The officer finally directed him to walk to the road. He was ordered to climb aboard the hood of a halftrack which had white and red stripes and was most likely a medical supply vehicle for the German column. Lyle thought, "This is surreal." He was numb and could not believe what was happening to him.

The column began slowly moving once more but proceeding directly toward the American medical unit Lyle had just passed. Then "all hell broke loose" as the Germans opened fire on that unit. Tracers were lighting up the sky and soon coming from both directions. Lyle was sitting up on the front hood with no protection whatsoever. Soon the same officer who had captured him arrived and took him to another halftrack filled with men and radio equipment. Now at least he was inside of the vehicle. With the shooting intensifying the officer shouted for the driver to turn around. While attempting to do so the halftrack slid off the narrow road and for a moment was stuck. The driver finally succeeded and began passing the other vehicles. Then it abruptly stopped. The same officer slowly exited the halftrack and walked back to where Lyle was seated. This time he motioned for him to get out and walk into the nearby woods. "This is it." He thought. But soon they came upon a clearing containing two tents. There were at least two dozen German soldiers there but nothing happened. Lyle was put into one of the tents where he remained all night. He was never approached by the enemy soldiers.

As the morning of the 20th approached, the sounds of jeeps and trucks could be heard heading towards the German lines. They were filled with GIs captured the previous night. Lyle was ordered to board one of the trucks and the column continued north towards Bastogne. They passed a small hamlet with a sign that read "Malmendy". None of the soldiers realized it but on the 17th, three days prior, nearly 100 captured Americans had been executed here by an SS unit under the command of Colonel Pfeiffer. How lucky Lyle had been to be captured by an officer who actually tried to protect him, or so it appeared during the battle.

After spending two nights in a building in a railroad yard, the men set out again now marching through the heavy snow. It was very, very cold. The GIs had to walk on each side of the road to allow German trucks and foot soldiers to pass down the middle. Lyle noticed that many were very young, only 14 or 15 years of age. It was also obvious the Germans were short of fuel since many of the trucks were pulling other smaller vehicles.

Finally the men boarded a 40 x 8 boxcar and were taken by train deep into Germany. The car was so congested that the prisoners were forced to stand up for the entire journey. The stench of human excrement was almost too much to bear. On December 24th, a rather sunny day he recalls, the prisoners were taken from the train to a warehouse and remained for nearly two hours. American bombers attacked the nearby railroad yard and luckily none of the men were injured. Their destination was Stalag 4b where there was some food and a little heat as Lyle recalls. In February, a group of nearly one thousand prisoners, both American and British, departed the camp. For nearly a month these men marched through farm country and slept in barns. The food was poor with the exception of an occasional treat, some boiled potatoes, which tasted so good.

Near the end of March the prisoners arrived in Stalag 7b. It was still very cold, maybe 20 degrees, but here there was no heat in the barracks. At least they had blankets to provide some protection on the frigid nights. Lyle remembers the men passing the time picking lice off their bodies and pinching these insects until they cracked. While many prisoners in World War II received Red Cross parcels these men did not. The men noticed an old "swayback" horse outside the gate confined in a circular enclosure. One day the horse disappeared. The following day the prisoners enjoyed some warm soup, but everyone knew what was in it. These were the only two hot meals Lyle remembers having as a prisoner. The guards in this camp were not regular German soldiers but older conscripts from Poland and Czechoslovakia.

By April the sounds of gunfire from the west grew louder with every passing day. On the 18th, the German guards evacuated the camp leaving the men unguarded. On April 19, a Scottish armored unit liberated this camp. The prisoners were finally free.

After returning to the "good old USA" Lyle attended college on the GI Bill. He married, raised a family and had long career in education.

Another veteran I cared for, a Vietnam vet, recently told me about an older gentleman he played softball against. He said, "The guy used one of those real old baseball gloves, like you see in movies." He also said that, "He was a former POW and a patient of yours." It was Lyle.

Lyle had a hip replacement several years ago and needed to switch from playing outfield to catcher. Finally at 92 years of age, it became time to hang up his glove from the sport he had loved since childhood.

Lyle had somehow survived the war in spite of several very close calls. What haunts him even to this day is why so many men he served with made the ultimate sacrifice for their country and yet he was spared.

Top: Young Lyle near his truck. Bottom: MIA telegram to his parents.

Lyle with his wife Mary.

ALMOST MADE IT --
JOHN BARTEMUS

Big John listened carefully to the elderly veteran's story of evading the Germans for nearly a month before being captured and he smiled. He had been successful for nearly 6 months and needed only to walk a few more miles before reaching safety in Switzerland. Would his luck hold out? While many of those who served in World War II have unusual combat experiences, some are remarkably unique. John's adventure is certainly one of them.

John Bartemus had been raised in Concord, New Hampshire, and enjoyed both music and sports during his youth. He was actually good enough with the clarinet and saxophone to play in both the high school and college jazz bands. There was money to be made when John played at local dances. Summer trips to Lake Placid to work in country clubs and nightclubs were also profitable.

Soon after the United States entry into World War II, John felt the need to do his duty and he enlisted. While in college, John had developed an interest in CPT, civilian pilot training. He naturally felt that this was where he belonged, and therefore entered Air Cadet training. After it was determined that his eyesight was inadequate to be a pilot in the Air Force, John opted to become a navigator instead. He was transferred to Texas for combat flight training and assigned to a B-17 crew. The program lasted nearly

6 months. As a navigator, he would be responsible for guiding the plane and its young crew safely using technology that was rather crude by today's standards. Celestial navigation was used when there were no obvious landmarks to follow such as when they were flying at night.

In the early 40s, once crews had been assigned to a plane and begun their journey overseas, they would often attempt to fly over their hometown if this was possible. John was no different and after picking up a plane in St. Louis, the crew began their journey to Presque Isle, Maine. This was John's opportunity to fly over his hometown and high school. One member of John's crew dropped a roll of toilet paper out the window that his brother, George, was able to see drifting slowly to earth.

The next stop would be Gander, Newfoundland. Bad weather, however, forced the crew to remain there for nearly 3 weeks. One afternoon, John's copilot went out for a ride on an A-26 with another pilot for some horsing around, just to kill time. Around 6 p.m., there was a great deal of commotion and John discovered that there had been an accident. The plane had clipped wings with a Canadian plane and John's copilot had been killed. The entire crew felt terrible losing their friend who unfortunately had a wife and child back home. The crew remained at the base for three more weeks until a replacement copilot arrived.

The next leg of their journey began but now things were different. They were flying with no more landmarks and in total darkness so the crew had to depend completely on John's ability to guide the plane safely to Scotland. John recalls that the enlisted men were quite impressed when he succeeded. Their flight was actually pleasant since they were able to fly at a comfortable 10,000 feet where oxygen masks were unnecessary.

Upon arriving, their plane was taken to a modification center to prepare it for battle but the plane was unfortunately damaged. A new B-17 was therefore needed. Eventually, John and the rest of the 10 man crew arrived in Ipswich, England, and became new members of the 385th Bomb Group. Practice missions were soon followed by the "real deal." The first four sorties were routine although they experienced some flak and attacks by enemy fighters. Luckily, no one was injured. Their next trip, during November of 1943, would be more memorable for the men since they were scheduled to bomb a chemical plant in southern Germany. The mission would take nearly 8 hours.

The pilot was flying at about 30,000 feet when he noticed that they were losing oil pressure in one engine which soon failed. They were forced to leave the formation and turn 180° when a second engine ceased to operate. Normally when an engine is lost it is immediately feathered so that the propellers cut through the air rather than cause drag. One engine could not be feathered however and, with the strong head wind that was encountered, airspeed quickly declined. All the heavy objects had to be discarded immediately. The bombs were the first to go and they were released over a wooded region so as not to injure any civilians. Flak suits and most of the ammunition followed. Some of the 50 caliber ammo was kept for the tail and top turrets. John soon heard the man in the top turret cut loose as about six FW 190s attacked the disabled plane. That man was promptly killed by a direct hit that spattered his remains everywhere. "It was pretty gruesome," John recalls.

With the plane now out of control and rapidly losing altitude, the pilot said it was time to "bail out" and he was the first to exit the plane. Other men followed. John climbed up into the cockpit to help and found that only the copilot remained. He was attempting to control the descending plane. Since they were now flying at only about 500 feet, it was apparent that bailing out was no longer an option. The copilot said they were going to crash land. He saw that they were approaching a plowed field and decided to go for a landing there. For John it was a very smooth landing in spite of the conditions. Since there was no landing gear used, these two remaining crewmembers only had to jump out of the windows to reach the ground. After an unsuccessful attempt to scuttle the plane by igniting leaking oil, they started to run since the first hour after crashing was critical for avoiding capture.

Soon they saw some approaching French civilians and two identified themselves as members of the underground. All those years studying French in high school and college were about to become very important for John. Both airmen were given civilian clothes and taken to a farmer's barn. They were directed to hide in the hayloft. Shortly a car could be heard approaching, a German staff car. The farmer went to the car and began speaking with the German soldiers. They were obviously satisfied with what he had to say and departed. Can you imagine the feelings of these two fugitives when they saw the Germans leaving without ever searching the premises?

John and his copilot were separated with each going to different French homes. The owner of John's residence was a repairman of sorts who operated out of a storefront in the building. He could repair a variety of items, even radios. He obviously had a good reputation and even did work for German soldiers who arrived at his store periodically, all while John was hiding nearby. The family fed him well and his French improved considerably during the stay.

After nearly 3 months of living with the family, it was time to move on with the idea of ultimately reaching Spain. One night, he and some of the other Allied airmen who were being hidden by the underground, were loaded onto a truck to begin their journey. Because of the blackout they could not use the headlights on the truck. After a brief ride, they collided with another truck stopped in the road. The truck full of German soldiers had a flat tire... The driver of John's truck jumped out and rushed forward to complain about their causing the accident. This was just enough distraction for John and the other men to jump out and sneak back to their houses.

The next attempt to leave was during the daytime when John boarded a bus for Lille, Belgium near the French border. The underground had provided John a fake ID and he got a room in a hotel for the night. Soon there was a knock at the door arousing John who promptly answered it. To his amazement there stood a German officer. "Can you give me the directions to the brothel?" John answered, "It's on the next floor,"

The plan was for John to board a train destined for Paris the next day. He was advised not to speak to anyone while on route. Once in Paris, the underground placed him in an apartment with three other men, two American GIs and the third an RAF fighter pilot. They lived on the second floor and had to spend most of their time inside to avoid detection. John recalls making a Monopoly game to control the boredom. Sundays however were special in that the men were allowed to take walks around Paris. Another close call occurred on one of these outings when John felt a nudge in his back. When he spun around there was a German soldier. Surely this was it he thought. But just as his anxiety was increasing, the soldier asked him directions to the train station. In his best French, John provided the answer. How many more close calls would there be? His stay in Paris lasted two more months until the decision was made to abort on the plan for Spain and attempt to reach Switzerland instead.

While in this grand city, John was reunited with his tail gunner.

One day, they were directed to board a train destined for Belfort, France. Once there, they would only have to walk the remaining few miles to freedom. At one farmhouse, John asked where they were. The woman answered but added that there were Germans everywhere. It was daylight. Should they continue walking or wait until nightfall? The decision was made to continue since they were so close to the border.

They walked for a while but soon it became very warm. Both were thirsty and exhausted and decided to stop at another farmhouse to obtain some fresh water. As they were approaching they heard someone shout," halt!" They spun in the direction of the harsh command only to see the barrels of rifles pointed in their direction. The three German soldiers had them. They were so close to freedom, ready to cross the border only to be captured by the enemy. They had gotten careless. It was now May 11, 1944, and their journey had ended.

John first heard threats that they would be shot as spies and saboteurs since they were not in uniform. They were shipped to Paris by train to a prison run by the feared Gestapo. Here the men slept on straw mattresses infested with fleas and had only a bowl of watery soup each day. At the Gestapo headquarters, the interrogator began to ask questions about the mission for which he already had the answers, to see if John was in fact an airman as he claimed. "Is there a circle, square or triangle on your plane?" was the question. John answered, "A square". "Is there a letter in the square?" "There is a G." He already knew the bomb group John was from and luckily concluded that he was telling the truth. "You, Lieutenant, are not a spy."

John did not realize it at the time, but how lucky he was that the German had agreed that he was in fact an enemy soldier and not a spy. Many airmen who had been hidden by the resistance during the war and who no longer had their dog tags, were considered spies and sent to Buchenwald concentration camp.

John was next shipped to Frankfurt for interrogation, again by the Gestapo. There he was kept in solitary confinement. He doesn't know how he survived this for he was very claustrophobic.

During the train ride through Berlin, he watched the city being bombed. The Allies were obviously closing in. On May 15, John finally arrived at this prison camp on the Baltic Sea in northern Germany. Stalag Luft 1 would be his home for the next year.

The rooms in the prison camp were crowded with 16 men sleeping on double bunks. There was some diversion with the sports they were allowed to play but what really saved John was the opportunity to form a prison band. They somehow obtained instruments and began practicing in the mess hall. This was a building where the food from the Red Cross parcels was being prepared. They could practice during the week and then entertain other prisoners at this mess hall on weekends. What a great release for the airmen held captive there. All of this ended when the mess hall caught fire and was destroyed, along with the instruments stored there.

By this time when it became apparent to the Germans that they were "getting licked", in John's words, and treatment of the Allied prisoners was not as harsh. The prisoners were one day visited by the former heavyweight champion, Max Schmeling, the German who had beaten Joe Louis early in his career. Being a German, his success as a fighter had been useful to Adolf Hitler when he boasted of Aryan supremacy. Max autographed various items for the prisoners including one that John has to this very day. "His hands were the size of baseball gloves," John remembers.

Finally in May of 1945, the camp was liberated by the Russians. John was flown to camp "Lucky Strike" at La Havre, France, for a brief recovery. While there he managed to borrow a car and returned to the home of the family that had dared hide him for nearly 3 months. When he arrived, all that was left was a hole in the ground, a bomb crater and the people had all been killed. How ironic that these people who had helped him had perished while he who had so many close calls had somehow survived.

John passed away a while ago. Of all the people included in this book, John was the only veteran who was not actually a patient of mine but a veteran I became acquainted with at one of the POW/MIA recognition events. His story is so unique and interesting, that it needed to be included. What a remarkable story! What a remarkable person!

Big John as a young airman.

The orchestra in the POW camp. John is seated second from the right.

Autograph of the former heavyweight champion Max Schmeling

John proudly wearing his Air Corps hat.

"BUSTER" --MAURICE SULLIVAN

The Normandy invasion on June 6, 1944, many consider to be the turning point in World War II in Europe. I for one, have always been intrigued by the events that transpired on D-Day and in August of 2015, visited this historic site. Attempting to land on these fortified beaches must have been a terrifying experience for those young men on that morning over 70 years ago. During my time caring for patients at the Veterans Administration Hospital, I spoke with hundreds of veterans of this war but very few who participated in this specific battle, but one day I met Maurice Sullivan, better known as "Buster".

Maurice was born and raised on a farm near Governor, New York, along with a younger brother and older sister. He had what he describes as a "good life" on that farm where he helped draw hay for the cows and horses and cultivate the fields. There were no huge tractors for his family; the fields were prepared with a one bottom plow all pulled by a single horse. His sister and Buster alternated walking behind the plow. While his younger brother loved to go fishing, Buster hated it. "They did not get any bites. There were a lot of it excuses but no fish," he recalls.

His education took place in a one room schoolhouse where all eight grades were crammed together. The teacher was actually able to teach all of the subjects to the students and be successful. Buster had to walk to school each day but he feels he received a "good education". Can you imagine children learning today under these conditions?

Buster enlisted in the Army in the summer of 1943 and completed basic training at Camp Swift in Texas. His next stop was for additional training in Missouri where he claims "nobody liked the first sergeant."

After traveling by ship to England, his company spent the next few months continuing to train. He recalls sleeping in eight-man tents during these months. The men knew they were preparing for something big but did not know what it would be.

Buster remembers crossing the English Channel in total darkness; the ships were totally blacked out. He was a member of the 4th Infantry Division, 8th Regiment scheduled to land at the western end of the Normandy beach, also known as Utah Beach. Buster did not realize it at the time, but he was about to participate in the largest invasion ever conducted during wartime.

There were about 30 men on his particular LCVP (Landing Craft, Vehicle, Personnel) also known as a "Higgins boat". Just after daybreak, the boat piloted by Navy personnel began slowly making its way toward shore. There were shells coming in but Buster remembers the driver saying he would "Go ashore so as not to get everyone wet." As the boat landed and the ramp was lowered, the vessel got stuck on the beach. The men had to "push him off so he could return for more soldiers."

Buster had two thoughts as all this was happening; "We are all in this together" and "Get off the beach as fast as we can." He remembers moving over a small rise and they immediately "were in trouble." There was "a lot of fire" coming from the enemy above. "It was terrible" Buster recalls. "The beach was all red with blood."

Buster claims they actually had landed about 1 mile from where they had intended to land but this occurred with most of the units landing that morning. They had managed to get through the huge fortifications the Germans had planted on the beaches as well as the tangles of barbed wire. The shelling from the huge ships offshore hammering the German fortifications had been deafening but not that effective.

Buster paused for a moment as he shared this portion of his Normandy memories with me. He said "I've tried to forget this experience." Hearing his description of what transpired that morning, this is understandable.

"By nightfall things were calming down." Buster recalls. They fought their way around the enemy and "got behind" them. Contact with the Germans continued. The men were exhausted having gone two or three days without sleep. After the beach, "The worst part was being so tired." Some of the troops attempted to sleep in the hedgerows inland from the beach but the Germans were hiding there also. There was one time when Buster was standing near one of these hedgerows when a German plane attacked. The plane swooped down and strafed the defenseless soldier but luckily the shells hit on either side of him. "I was much thinner then," Buster laughs.

The troops slowly fought their way northwest of their landing site to the French city of Cherbourg. After battling the Germans there, the American troops slowly began making their way down the streets of the city. There was "nobody in the streets" according to Buster "but as soon as we went through, the civilians came outside."

The Germans had a naval school in Cherbourg. While on the second floor of the building, Buster found a portrait of Adolf Hitler hanging on the wall. He took it down and threw it out the window onto the street below. The picture landed with Hitler staring up. A few minutes later a woman approached and examined the portrait. Before walking away, she urinated on the portrait.

After two long months in combat, Buster and his unit were fighting near Saint Pois. While the enemy was retreating, they continued to fight fiercely. In addition to his responsibilities as an infantryman, Buster was also tasked with maintaining communication lines by laying out and repairing the wires when necessary. One day when the American troops had retreated a bit, Buster continued to work on the repairs when a shot rang out. He was hit in the leg. Though seriously injured, he was alert enough to see two German soldiers approaching. Once they reached him, they dropped their weapons. They obviously had had enough and used this as an opportunity to surrender to an American.

What was really strange to Buster was that they did not want to be separated from him. When help arrived, the Germans said, "We will take care of him." The Germans helped load him on the Jeep and climbed aboard. As Buster puts it, "They wanted out of there." The day of his injury ironically was his birthday, August 5.

While recovering from the wound in a hospital in England, Buster was surprised to hear a familiar voice. "Buster, what are you doing here?" It was a girl from Ogdensburg, New York, who was a close friend of his older sister and now working as a nurse. "What a small world," Buster concluded.

After being discharged from the Army on his birthday one year later, he returned to civilian life. Soon he got married and began a family like most of the other men who survived the war.

In spite of the smile that always appeared on Buster's face, I can never forget his final words on the date of this interview. "I hope nobody ever has to go through this again."

Buster was one of several patients who usually traveled some distance for their dental care. Often this meant that they actually passed other VA hospitals feeling more comfortable with our clinic.

I usually arranged for a late afternoon appointment for an examination and cleaning but reserved time early the next day if more work was necessary. Many of these veterans would travel with their wife and make this a mini getaway/vacation.

One Vietnam patient I will not forget came from Canton with his wife and asked where they might stay and have a nice dinner that evening. I made suggestions and said that there was even a "Dick's" store near the restaurant.

The following morning when I greeted the veteran in the waiting room however he was not smiling. I said, "What's wrong?"

He replied firmly. "You didn't tell me that there was a huge mall across from Dick's. Once my wife got in the mall, she had to shop until they closed."

German bunkers above the Normandy Beaches.

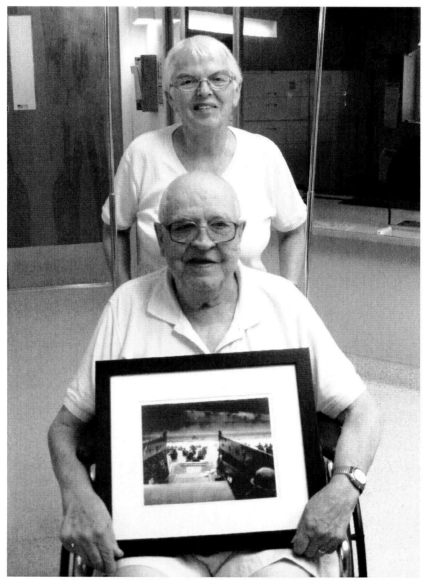

Buster in the waiting room with his wife and smiling as usual.

P-47 -- RICHARD BEDFORD

Each year all former prisoners of war and servicemen listed as missing in action are recognized at ceremonies throughout the United States on MIA/POW recognition day. I have been honored to be invited to the event held in Rochester, New York, for several years because of my association with many veterans who are also former POWs. A few years ago, I was introduced to Richard Bedford by Donald Barton who stated that Mr. Bedford's military experiences were very different from most of the other veterans I had met in the past. A pilot from Don's bomb group in the Eighth Air Force named Roy Allen had been shot down on a combat mission over Europe and spent the remainder of the war imprisoned with Dick Bedford but not in a POW camp such as Stalag Luft III. These airmen had not been so fortunate. They were sent to the concentration camp known as Buchenwald. One day I asked Mr. Bedford if he would share some of his experiences with me. He replied that after many years of not talking about the war that nothing was "off limits" any longer. What follows is the story of a very brave man who demonstrated the limits of human endurance during his ordeal.

Richard was born in 1922 to teenage parents in the inner city of Rochester, New York, and grew up poor as many people did during the Great Depression. He remembers that this family was on "welfare" during those lean years. While sports did not really interest him, his involvement with the Boy Scouts was special. Active for many years he achieved the rank of "Eagle Scout" as a teenager, an accomplishment he is very proud of to this day.

After high school, he began working at Kodak and met a chemist who would later give him flying lessons. He loved flying and after Pearl Harbor decided to join the military and become a fighter pilot.

At that time anyone who wanted to fly would have to have gone to college for at least two years. Since the war had begun and so many airmen had been lost in combat, this requirement could be waived if a rigorous examination could be passed. Richard did so and was on his way to becoming an aviation cadet. He was sent to Avon Park, Florida, to begin his primary flight training. After only five hours of instruction in this first plane, he was able to fly solo. From there it was on to Macon, Georgia, and training on the BT-13 (basic trainer), the first plane with a two pitch propeller. At Spence Field he trained with the AT-6 (advanced trainer) and ultimately the P-40. This was the first plane with no "duel time" meaning no instructor was on board. Each aircraft was becoming more advanced and complex with each step in the process. In August 1943, he graduated from single engine training and was now a second lieutenant. While on leave, he and his girlfriend Doris became engaged.

While Dick enjoyed flying the P-40, its limited range was not suited for combat missions in Europe. In Tallahassee, Florida, he was introduced to the twenty eight hundred horse power P-47 Thunderbolt and his training began with the plane he would ultimately fly in combat. In November, 1943, Richard and Doris were married and were allowed to live off base. One day he arrived and found that the base had been "locked down." He was to be shipped out without even telling Doris goodbye. After traveling to Boston, he was put on a ship bound for England where he would become a replacement pilot. At that time the P-38, P-47, and P-51 fighters were being used in combat missions over Europe. Richard and his friend Art decided that the fighter group with the fewest openings must be losing fewer pilots and chose the 353 Fighter Group that needed two men. After training with this group for one month, it was time to begin real combat missions. Escorting bombers such as the B-17, B-24, B-25, and B-26 on their missions to bomb Germany would be his initial responsibility.

After meeting in the briefing room early in the morning on the day of a mission for instructions, the pilots would take off as a squad. While the top speed was 450 mph, they usually would fly at 280 to 300 mph, and catch up with the much slower bombers (135 mph) somewhere over the North Sea. One hundred percent radio silence was the absolute rule. The P-47 had eight 50 caliber machine guns, four per wing, and could also carry bombs when necessary. The fighters would fly above the bombers and zig zag because of their greater flying speed. While enemy fighters were always a threat, the greater danger was from enemy flack exploding all around the planes. The enemy used the very accurate 88 mm artillery piece whose projectile was set to detonate and spray shrapnel into nearby planes. Many men lost their lives during the war as the result of the German anti-aircraft. The bombers were always at greater risk than the fighters since they had to stay in tight formations and not take evasive action. With their limited fuel however, the P-47 fighters could only provide protection to Germany.

Once the P-47 descended lower to tree top level and was "on the deck", it rarely would climb to a higher altitude. When returning from one mission and flying on the deck, Richard's closest friend and wing man Art Bergeron was blown up by flack. This was his first exposure to the pain of losing a friend in combat and was a scene he would never forget.

Over the next few months the combat missions continued. Richard knew he would be eligible to return to the states after completing fifty missions, but this changed on D-day. This would be his first mission flying in the dark (4 a.m.) on what would prove to be a historic day. He was very close to other planes, but he could see only their exhaust trails. The sky was lit up like the fourth of July as they approached the Normandy coast of France. Each streamer shooting up through the darkness ended with a flash. These were not holiday fireworks, however. During all of his daylight missions, there had been only the dark puff from exploding enemy flack. The plane's wings had each been painted with three white stripes for quick identification by other Allied forces and were not yet dry. There were so many ships below that you could have walked to shore. This was an "unbelievable undertaking" with such a huge number of ships, fighter planes and C-47 transport planes towing gliders. He could still see the beachhead from inland where he was strafing and bombing targets of opportunity. This was the first of three such missions flown on that memorable day that would change the course of the war in Europe.

After D-Day, the missions were all to engage and destroy targets of opportunity in France to support the advancing Allied forces. The most memorable mission, however, would be his 65th on June 12, 1944. On this morning (D-Day + 6) at approximately 0415 hours, he took off for a regular mission to patrol for "Jerry" convoys with 15 other Allied fighters. At about 0530, the squadron was attacked by approximately 25 ME 109 German fighters at an altitude of 6000 feet. This was a "good fight" as Richard put it but "he lost." He knows he got at least one Me109 and damaged another before being hit and catching fire. Richard bailed out at between 3000-5000 feet and landed rather hard in a field. The first person he met was Pierre Tidow, a farmer from Eure, France. He later learned that eight planes had been shot down and five men killed on that particular mission.

The farmer fed him, gave him civilian clothes, and told him to hide in the nearby woods and Pierre would return when it became dark. At around 10 p.m., Richard was fed again and given a map of the area roads along with a French/English translation book. He began to walk northwest and continued for most of the night except for a brief nap in a cold, wet field. In the morning he began walking again and ate some more of the food provided by Pierre. At nearly 5 p.m., Richard met another person and decided to ask for help. He was taken to city hall and met the mayor. A guide was provided to take him to a farm where he would spend the night. On the following day, Richard was again escorted to another farm that would become his home for the next six weeks.

This family consisted of the farmer, his wife, two children and the in-laws. They treated him well and provided excellent food. French lessons were provided by the "professor" and he spent much of his time reading and working in the garden. On July 2, the enemy took over part of the house for several days and Richard was forced to hide in a shack in the woods nearby. After he returned to the house, there were frequent scares from "Goons" (informers) sneaking around.

On July 20, Richard was taken to Paris, against his better judgment, by a red haired woman from Belgium and her friend "Jacques". The understanding was that he would then escape through Switzerland or Spain to be reunited with his fighter group. He became suspicious when the car in which he was riding was allowed through roadblocks. Jacques Desoubrie was actually from Belgium and spoke several languages. It was later learned that this double agent received 10,000 francs for every airman he turned over to the Germans. After the war, Jacques was convicted of war crimes and executed. His last words were, "Heil Hitler."

Richard was put up in an apartment where he was fed and even obtained a bike to tour Paris for a few days. Little did he know that he had been betrayed by Jacques and on July 23 at 11 p.m., he was arrested by the Gestapo. These three men in civilian clothes said, "For you, the war is over." He was taken to the Gestapo headquarters on the Avenue Foch for interrogation. In all, 168 Allied airmen (82 Americans) were arrested and identified as "Terror Fleigers (Air Gangsters) or Saboteurs". The only thing he had to identify himself as an Allied airman, his dog tags, was taken by his captors and not returned. This was considered by many to be a "chamber of horrors." Moans and screams could be heard during the night. Richard however only recalls being hit with a rubber truncheon on the head during these hours of interrogation.

The following day, July 24, he was taken to Fresnes Prison just outside of Paris. It was one of the most famous of all the French prisons. Here Richard was searched, deloused, and thrown into a cell with three

French prisoners where they would remain for three weeks. During this time the fighting had continued in the hedgerows of Normandy and after two months, the "breakout" from the Cotentin Peninsula became eminent. When it became apparent to the Germans that Paris was about to fall to the Allies, the prisoners were transferred to a marshalling (railroad) yard to board trains. The 40x8 box cars (intended for 40 people or 8 horses) were loaded with nearly 100 prisoners each. There were two five gallon pails per car. One was filled with water, while the other was intended for human waste. This would soon be overflowing with so many men crammed into such a small boxcar. The men were held for five days in these cars under cramped, hot, and unsanitary conditions.

During their trip, the train attempted to pass through a long tunnel but the other opening had been blocked. The train simply stopped there and continue to belch steam and smoke. Some of the prisoners feared they might soon perish but after nearly two hours the train backed out. After helping to unload some equipment, the men boarded a second train.

One boy, about 16, attempted to look out one of the small vents covered with barbed wire and was shot in the hand. The next time the train stopped to allow the prisoners to relieve themselves this boy was taken away. The other prisoners assumed he would receive medical assistance but he was executed instead.

There was concern that the train might be strafed by Allied planes but Richard knew that they usually attempted to hit only the engine unless artillery pieces were being transported. The prisoners were resigned to the fact that they were going to prison camp. This was about to change when the train slowly entered the camp that was filled with "walking skeletons" wearing black and gray uniforms and with blank staring faces. These emaciated prisoners who appeared starved where in fact residents of "Koncentration Lager Buchenwald" or KLB.

One of the first structures evident to most of these new prisoners was the towering chimney from the crematorium. The smoke billowing from its top smelled like burned bacon and was continuous. The guards pointed at the chimney and told the men that the only way out of here is "up that chimney".

Buchenwald was constructed in 1937 as a concentration or labor camp like Dachau (1933). It was intended for political prisoners and contained factories utilizing the free labor. While not an extermination camp, over fifty thousand of the 250,000 people who were imprisoned there ultimately died from disease or starvation. Richard's KLB number would be 78283. After being stripped and shaved of all body hair, each prisoner was swabbed with a stinging disinfectant. A shirt and pair of pants, probably from someone who had died, were given to each man. No shoes or socks were provided. The prisoners were directed to sleep on the rocky ground and share one blanket between three men.

While Buchenwald had some regular German guards, the worst treatment came from the "Capos" who were privileged prisoners. They were very mean and administered regular beatings. Each day a roll call or "appell" would occur twice and this was repeated until all persons were accounted for.

The rations were meager. At 5 a.m. coffee/broth and a slice of bread made with sawdust and barley was provided. Later that day one more slice of this bread and a bowl of broth/soup were given for sustenance. The sanitary facilities consisted of an open trench/pit with a rail over the middle for support to prevent falling in during defecation. Richard used a scrap of his shirt to clean himself after using this open toilet. With time the toll of such sanitation and poor nourishment became evident as illness spread throughout the camp. Diarrhea and dysentery affected everyone. Five to ten bodies would be hauled daily to the crematorium; the result of disease and malnutrition.

A body would sometimes be left hanging as the result of an execution to set an example for the other prisoners. Death became a way of life for the living skeletons at Buchenwald.

The airmen tried to maintain some degree of military discipline in spite of this harsh treatment that led to the humiliation and degradation of other KLB prisoners. The highest ranking officer assumed "command" of the airmen. His name was Colonel Philip Lamason from New Zealand. He was the pilot of a British Lancaster Bomber. He provided some degree of leadership and all of the Allied airmen respected him. The men believed that they would somehow survive this horrible experience.

After one month of sleeping out on the cold damp earth, they were finally allowed to move into a barracks where enough of the inmates had died to make room for the new residents. The barracks had shelves/bunks where a row of six men slept with their heads exposed and feet to the wall to protect any footwear from theft. The shelves were four rows high. Twenty four men slept cramped in each section.

While other prisoners were forced to work, Lamason instructed the airmen to refuse. One day as a group of B-17s flew over, the men noticed that flares were being dropped directly on their camp. They were terrified for they all knew what would immediately follow. As it turned out, the target was the munitions factory at Buchenwald. Luckily, only this factory and some nearby structures were damaged but the Germans demanded that the airmen help fight the fires and salvage anything that could be saved. Walking through the burning rubble without any shoes was nearly impossible.

Members of the Luftwaffe (German Air Force) soon became aware of the fact that Allied airmen were mistakenly being imprisoned at KLB when they came for a visit. One of the American airmen, who spoke German, ran up to the officers and told the German that there were numerous Allied airmen being held prisoner there. One of the officers said, "This is no place for fellow flyers. We will do what we can."

Finally, on October 20, 1944, the Allied airmen were taken from Buchenwald. They had actually been scheduled for execution on the 24th. They had somehow avoided the fate suffered by 37 British SOE officers that were either shot or hung. Richard Bedford had lost 68 pounds during his stay in Buchenwald. The nightmare was over finally.

The decision was made to move these airmen to an appropriate prison in Sagon, Poland known as Stalag Luft III. This time their ride on the 40 X 8 boxcars was much less congested. The enemy airmen, the Luftwaffe, a "comrade in arms" had help save their lives.

On October 21, 1944, all surviving airmen (two had died in Buchenwald) arrived at a true POW camp. This is the same prison where earlier prisoners had attempted to escape by digging elaborate tunnels but had failed. They showered for the first time in months and were given clothes that included underwear and a pair of shoes. The other prisoners could not believe the poor physical condition of these men nor the stories that were shared about their experiences. Here the German guards were often older men and there was little abuse.

Richard would live here until January, 1945, when plans were made to evacuate the prison due to the advancing Russian army. His stay here had been like heaven after enduring Buchenwald. A postcard that he was finally allowed to send to this wife was the first information she received that he was actually alive. She had assumed that he was dead all of this time.

The prisoners were given only an hour's notice to depart on that cold snowy January night. Slats from the bunks were used to construct sleds to carry food and clothing for this next ordeal. Red Cross parcels that he had not seen in Buchenwald were received regularly at Stalag Luft III. Each man would be allowed to bring one half of a 10 pound Red Cross package to sustain him for this journey into Germany. At approximately 1:15 a.m., they left and marched all night and most of the following day. The men covered 37 km that first day enduring subzero conditions. The next day the men marched an additional 34 km (approximately 50 miles total). By the 31st of January they had covered 89 km. As of February 2, the men had marched 100 km or nearly 62 miles in five frigid days. Finally, they were loaded on a 40x8 boxcar and transported to Nurnberg arriving February

4, 1945. This movement from camp to camp continued off and on until on April 29, 1945, when their last camp at Moosburg was liberated by General Patton's army.

Richard eventually made his way to Camp Lucky Strike in France and then back to the states. He learned after returning home that some of the French people who had helped him were executed by the Germans.

He went on to have a successful career at Kodak and raised two daughters, Bonnie and Susan. Four grandchildren followed. His grandson, like Richard, was an Eagle Scout and later became a priest. He served as a prison chaplain in Nebraska. Two of his granddaughters became nuns with a teaching order also in Nebraska. The 4th granddaughter became a radiology technician. Dick Bedford is very proud to have such a wonderful family.

I asked him recently how he feels today after living through such an ordeal. He said he has no animosity towards the German people. When I asked if he ever wanted to fly a plane after his discharge from the service, he said, "I love to fly but I had had enough by the end of World War II."

I was asked by the Chatterbox Club (a 90 year old woman's club in Rochester, New York) of which my wife Debbie is a member, to bring a few of my special patients for a Veterans Day celebration two years ago with the hope that they would share some of their World War II experiences. One of the other special guests was a 90 year old lady who had flown bombers around the United States for delivery to their new crews. She and a few other gentlemen spoke and then it was Richard's turn. As he was speaking, I noticed some of the audience had tears in their eyes. When he had finished sharing this remarkable story of human cruelty, there was total silence. He slowly walked towards his seat. As he approached the lady pilot, she raised her hand. Richard stopped and grasped it. I cannot adequately describe my feelings but I am sure they were shared by all in attendance at that special moment.

Dick recently attended an airshow in Rochester, New York, and was privileged to be a passenger in a vintage P-51 fighter from World War II. They flew south over the Finger Lakes region of western New York. Being in the plane brought back a lot of memories for this old warrior. After landing, the first thing his daughter said however was how "cute" the young pilot was. Dick promptly told her that he was also "young and cute" at one time but that was when he was flying combat missions nearly seventy years ago.

Dick on the left with his buddy who lost his life on a mission shortly after the photograph was taken.

Dick Bedford's Buchenwald documents.

The entrance to Buchenwald.

The chimney at Buchenwald. The only way out.

The crematorium at Buchenwald.

Kriegsgefangenenlager

Datum: October 21 '44

Dearest Doris: - I know you've been sorta waiting for this 1st letter - Im safe And well as A war Prisoner - Hope you Are well - Tell everyone not to worry - TRy To send packages of candy DRIed And food To me - Lt R.L. BEDFORd 8126 STalag - Luft #3 - Germany - Will wRiTe As often As possible - Take care of youRself - Love

Dick

The first letter Dick's wife received after finally arriving at Stalag Luft III.

Surviving members of the Airmen of Buchenwald as
guests of the German government in 2014.

Dick holding the brochure from the Air Show depicting his P-47.

AFTERWORD

Growing up, I always had heroes. They were easy to find back then. I wanted to be an athlete so I had pictures of Mickey Mantle and Sam Huff on my wall, two sports figures who seemed to personify qualities I needed to develop if I wanted to succeed in sports. I think it was easier to be a hero before the 24 hour news cycle, and social media became part of our lives. The flaws of sports figures, actors, politicians, and successful people were not constantly revealed by a level of human frailty in a culture where everything one did was not known. Today, every time someone comes along who demonstrates some level of heroism, that person is immediately revealed to have serious flaws. The media builds people up, then tears them down. Real heroes are in short supply. Those who are encouraged to emulate seem to have too many blemishes, and too much behavioral baggage to be considered truly heroic. So, if heroes can be hard to find, where do we look to find individuals we can admire, or whose behavior we can strive to duplicate in our own lives?

In his book, Dr. Bastow has answered that question by recognizing that real heroes can often be found very close to home. The stories told to him by his dental patients reveal a level of heroism and dedication to duty exhibited by "regular people" who were placed in difficult situations and needed to respond in order to survive. In these stories, a common thread is the concept of duty, doing what one is expected to regardless of consequence. All his patients, when questioned about why they acted as they had, responded by saying, "I was just doing my job," or, "It was what was expected of me." Dr. Bastow has found the humility that these people brought to their situations. Most of them were reluctant to speak of what they had experienced, and did not see themselves as heroic in any sense. His book allows a look into how members of "the Greatest Generation" approached their service to country. They do not think that what they did is remarkable in any way. Humility is a characteristic clearly lacking in contemporary society. It is refreshing to read about people who consider their accomplishments to be "no big deal." The stories serve as confirmation that the humble man or woman next door to us may actually be more of a real hero than any person we see on television or read about in the media.

When their war was over, these people returned home and immersed themselves in life. They married, raised families, started businesses, worked hard, and made a place for themselves in society. They did not act like heroes, but continued to do their duty, forming a societal bedrock which helped our country develop and prosper. They took off their uniforms and restarted their lives even after experiencing hardship which could have broken those of less strength. In their stories, I see an affirmation of something I have always believed: ordinary people can accomplish extraordinary things.

The people who fought two wars, and established much of the basis of our society are leaving us every day. It has been over 70 years since the end of World War II, and as people die, their actions may never be known. Stories of real heroism never get old, and need to be told before they vanish. Dr. Bastow has made sure the stories of his patients are not forgotten. He has created a fitting tribute to their heroism and dedication to duty. Thank you, Jeff, for bringing these stories to light and for your ability to capture in your writing how extraordinary these ordinary people were and are.